PICTURE BOOK OF
CUTE CATS

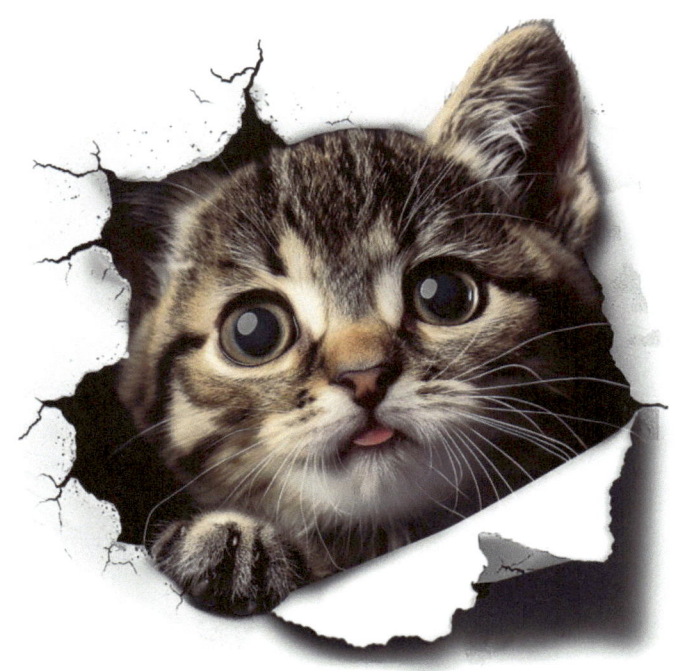

...By...
Ella Caldwell

Copyright © 2024. All rights reserved.

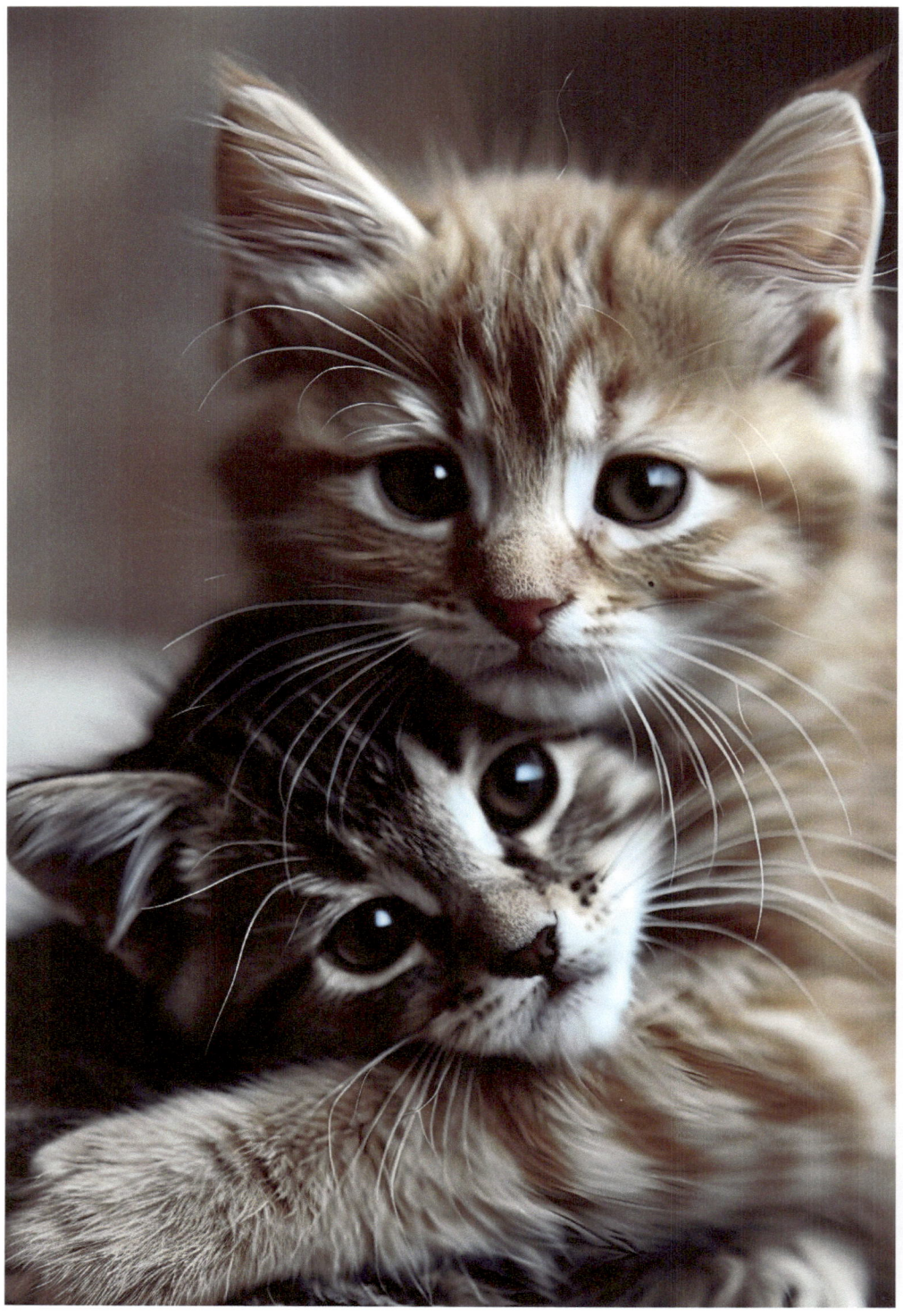

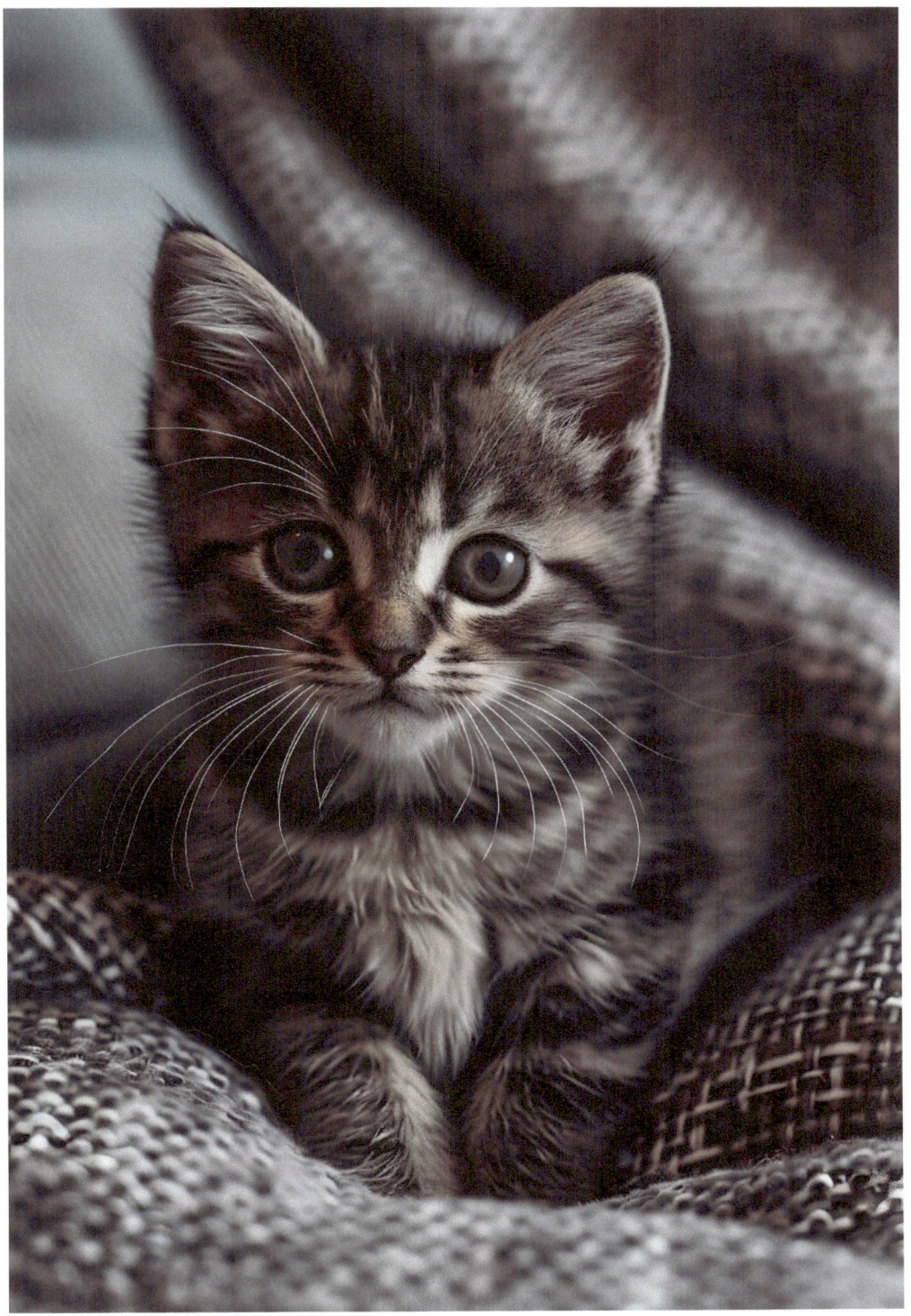

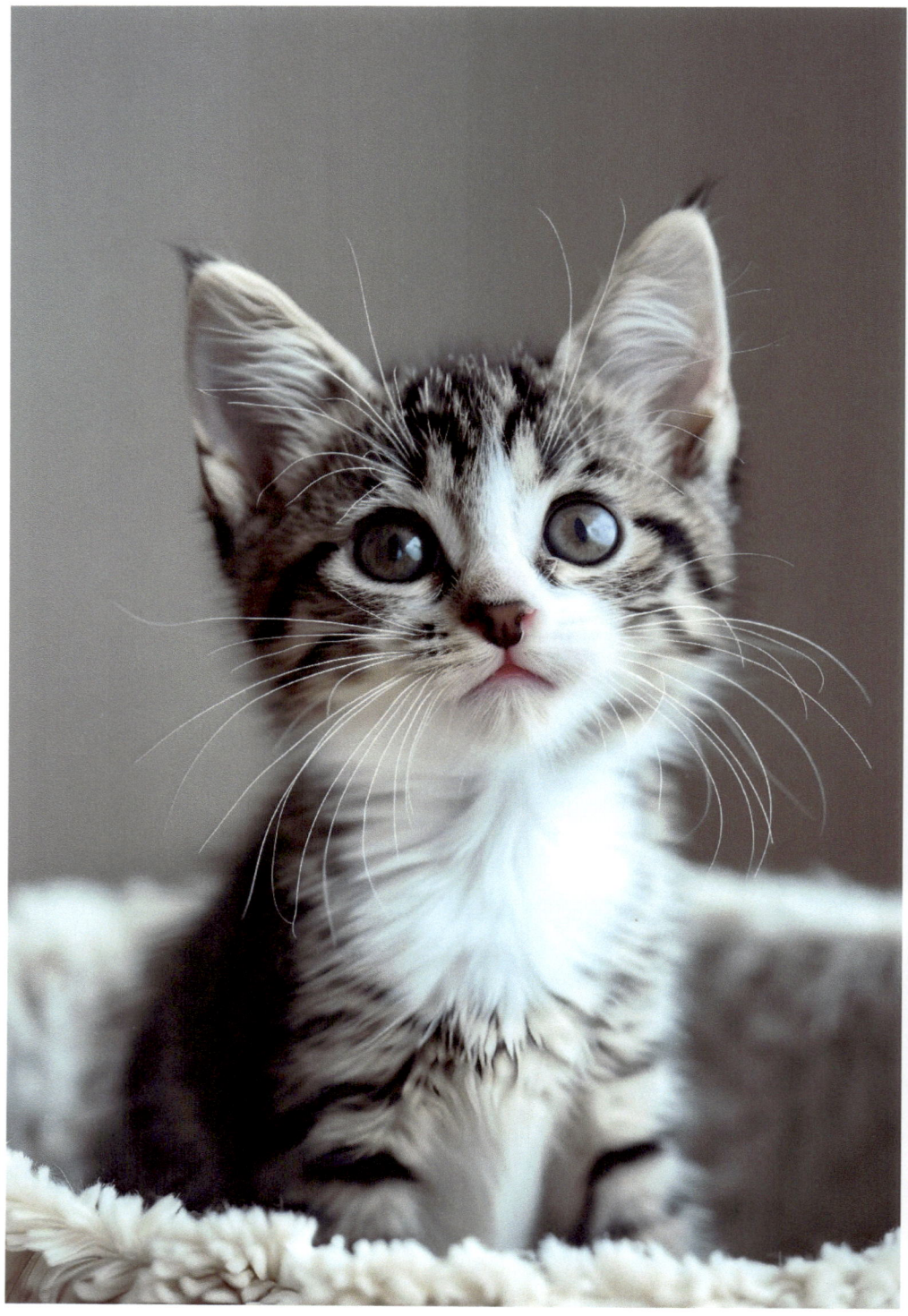

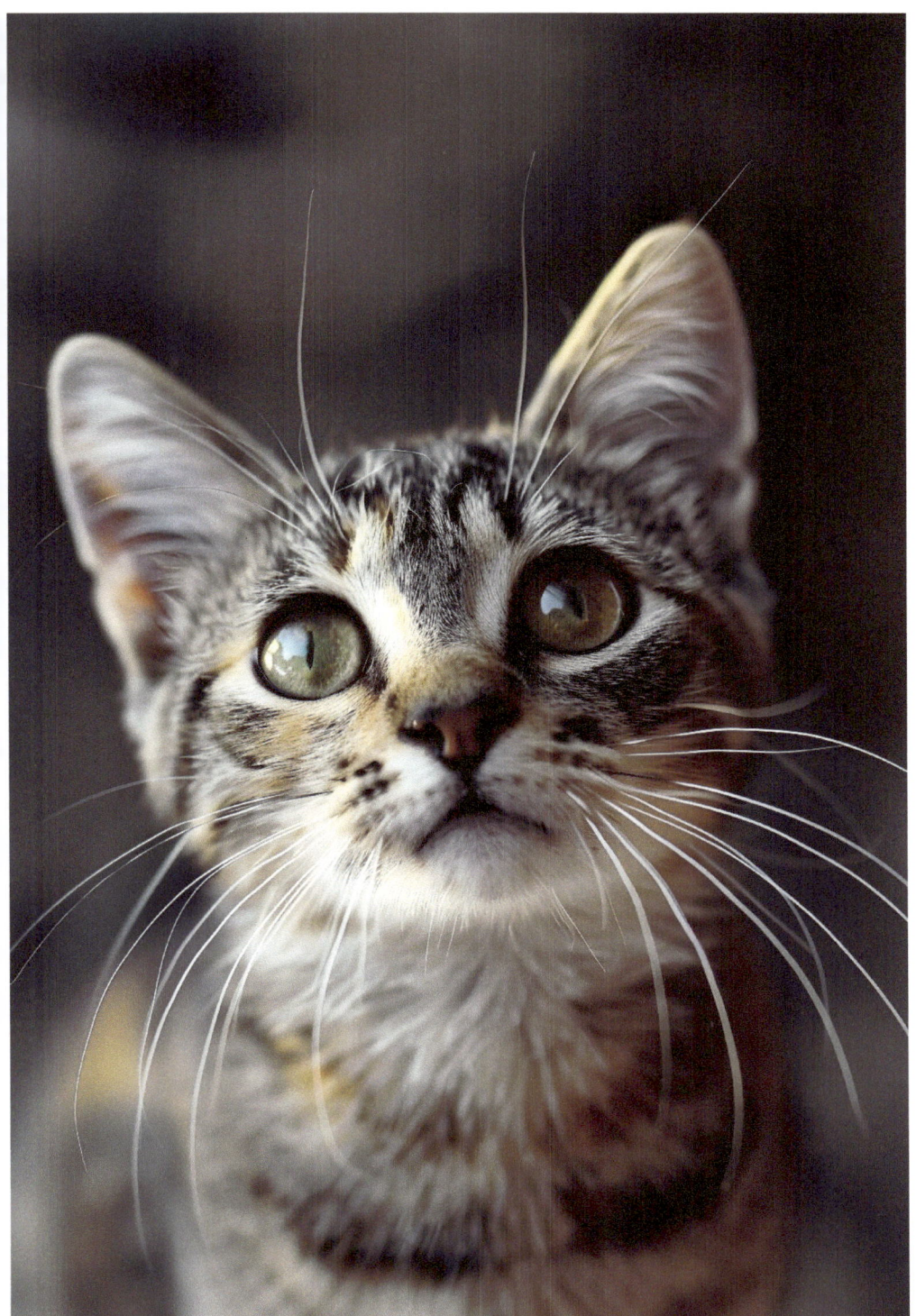

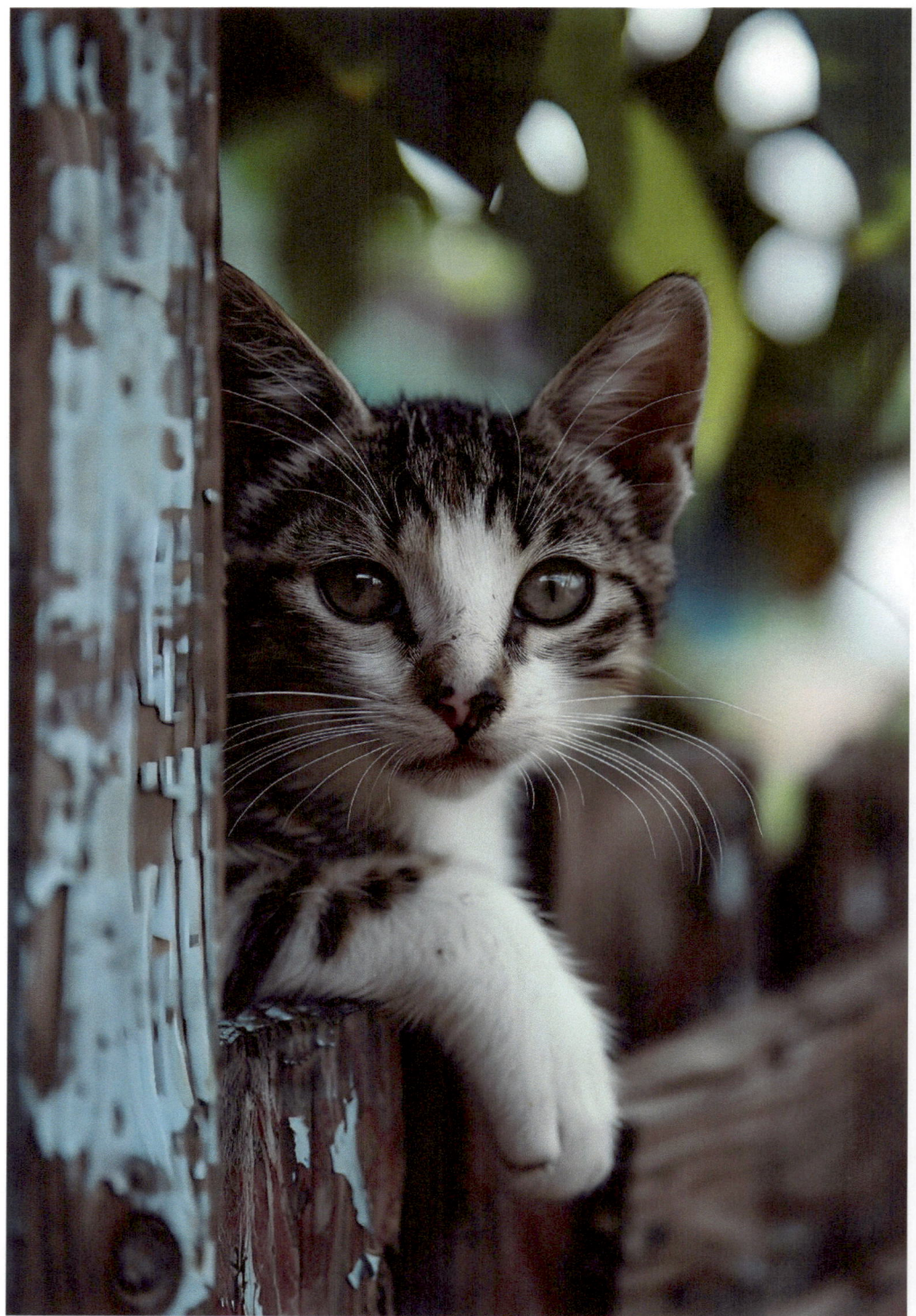

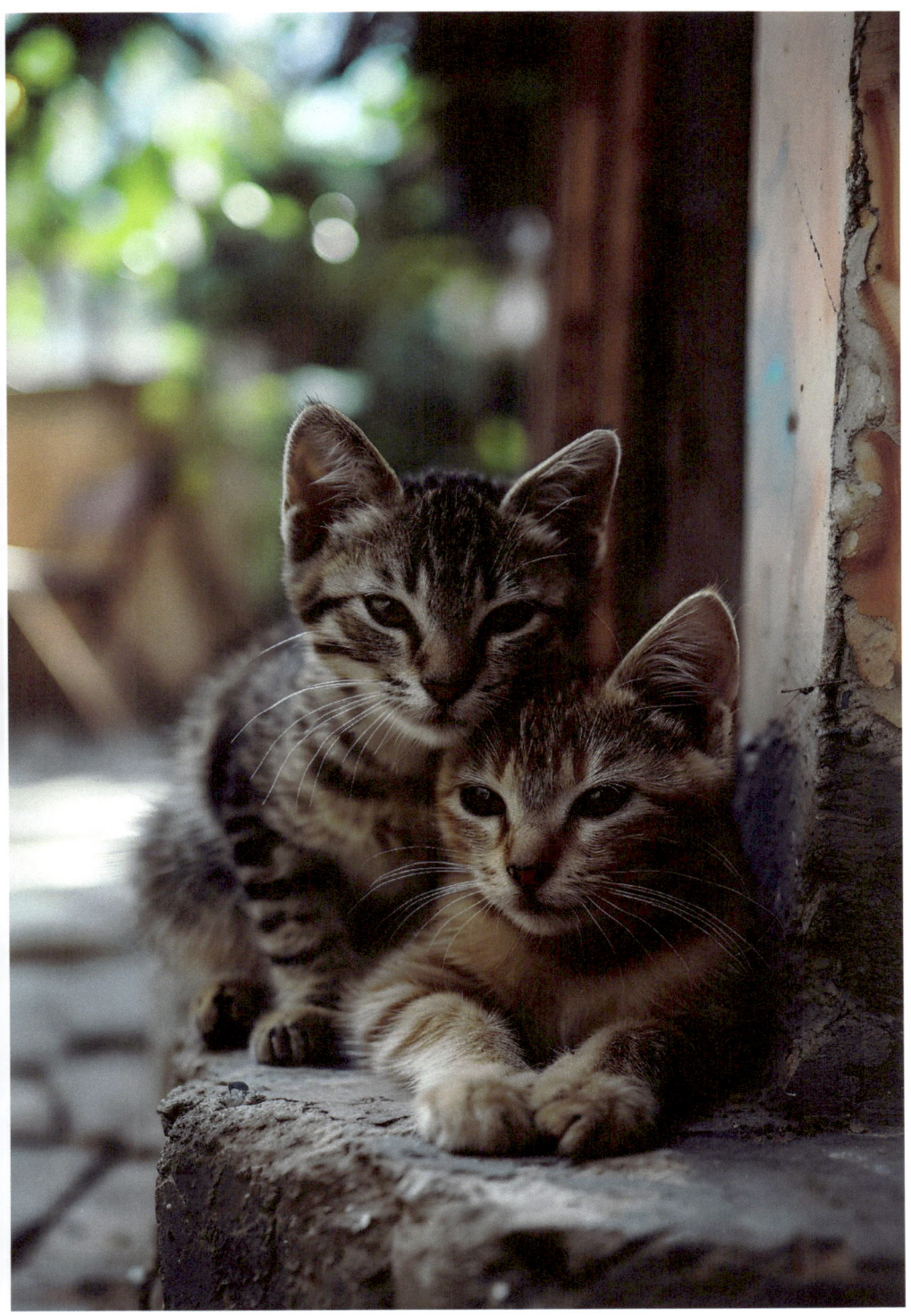

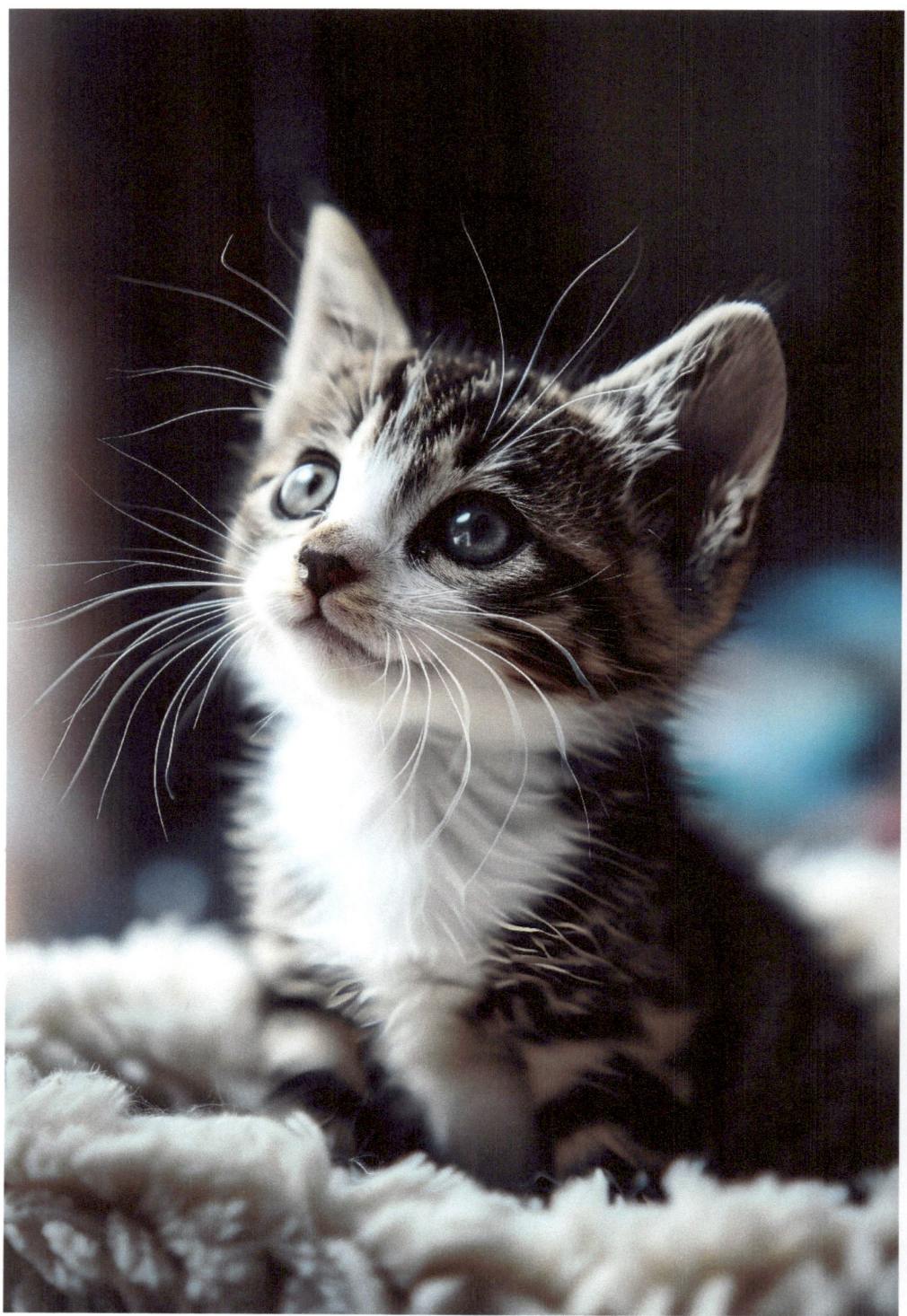

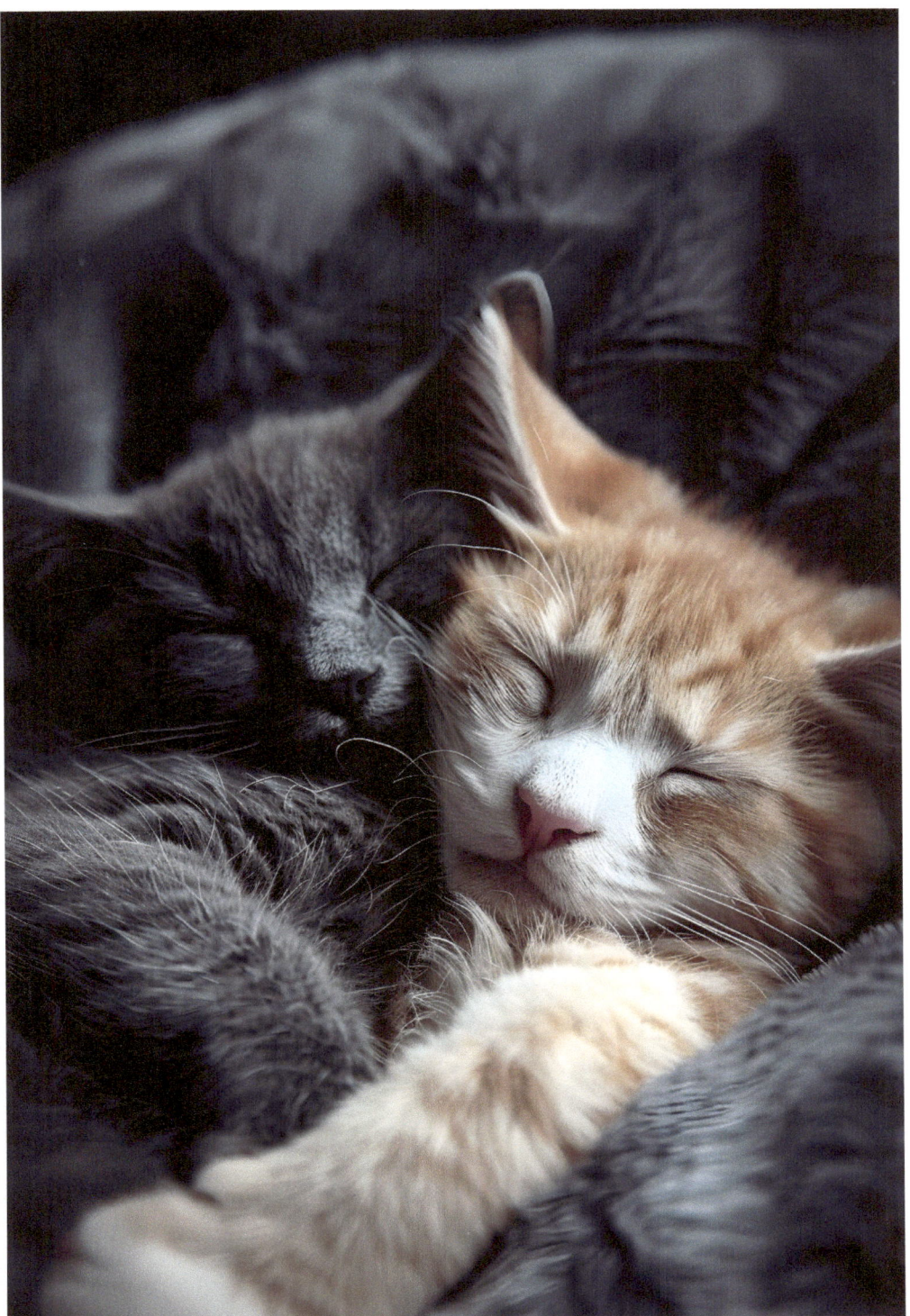

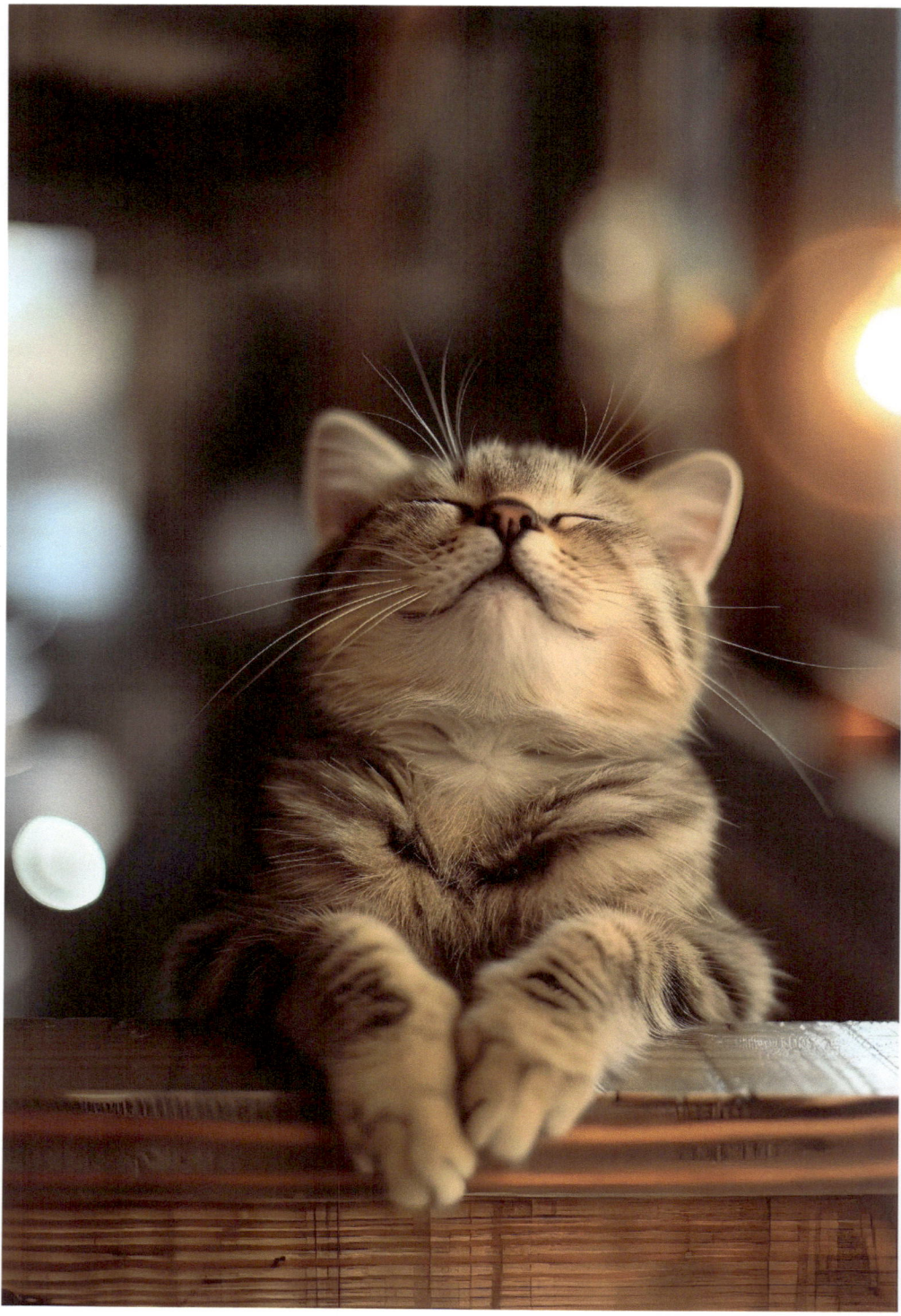

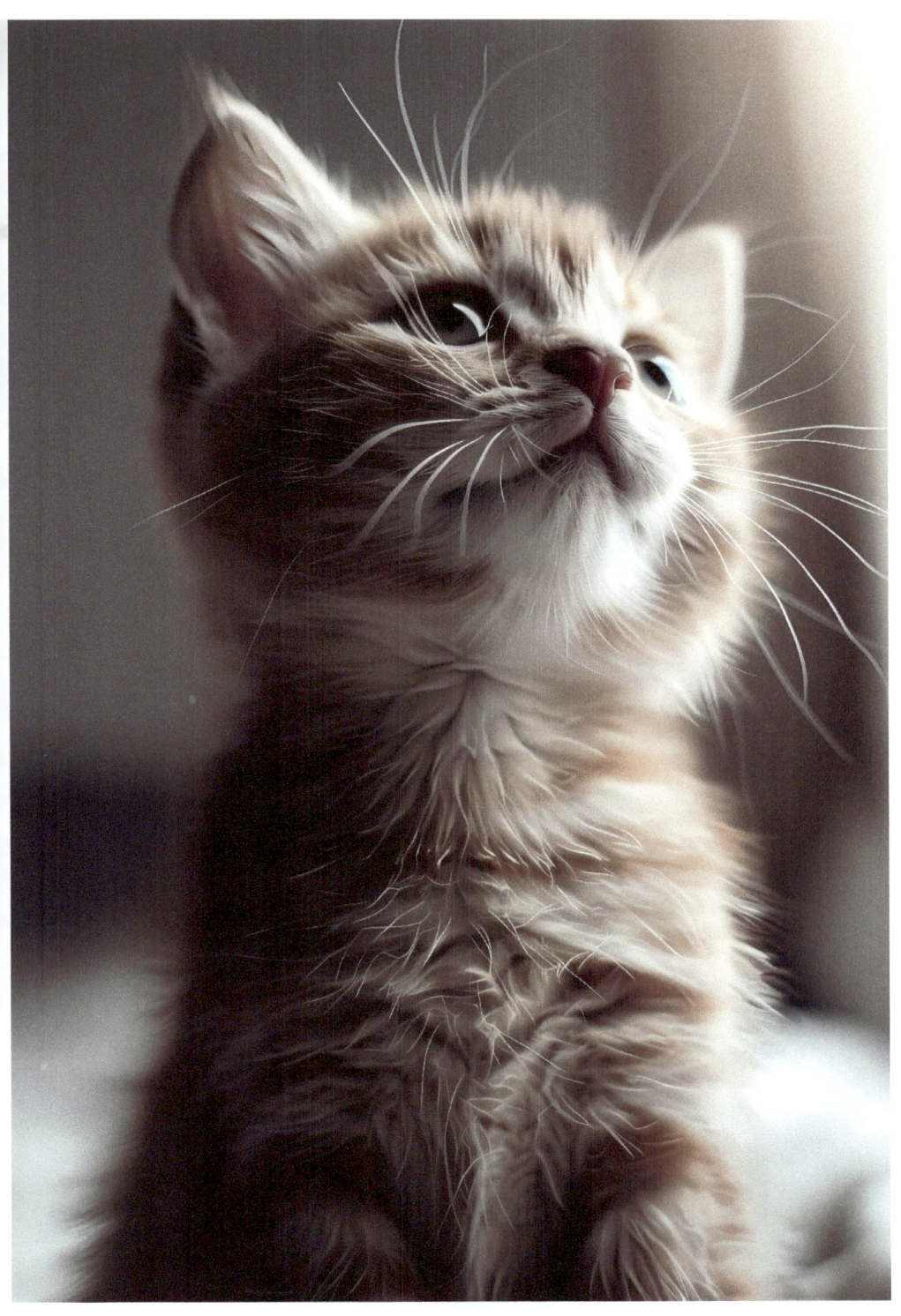

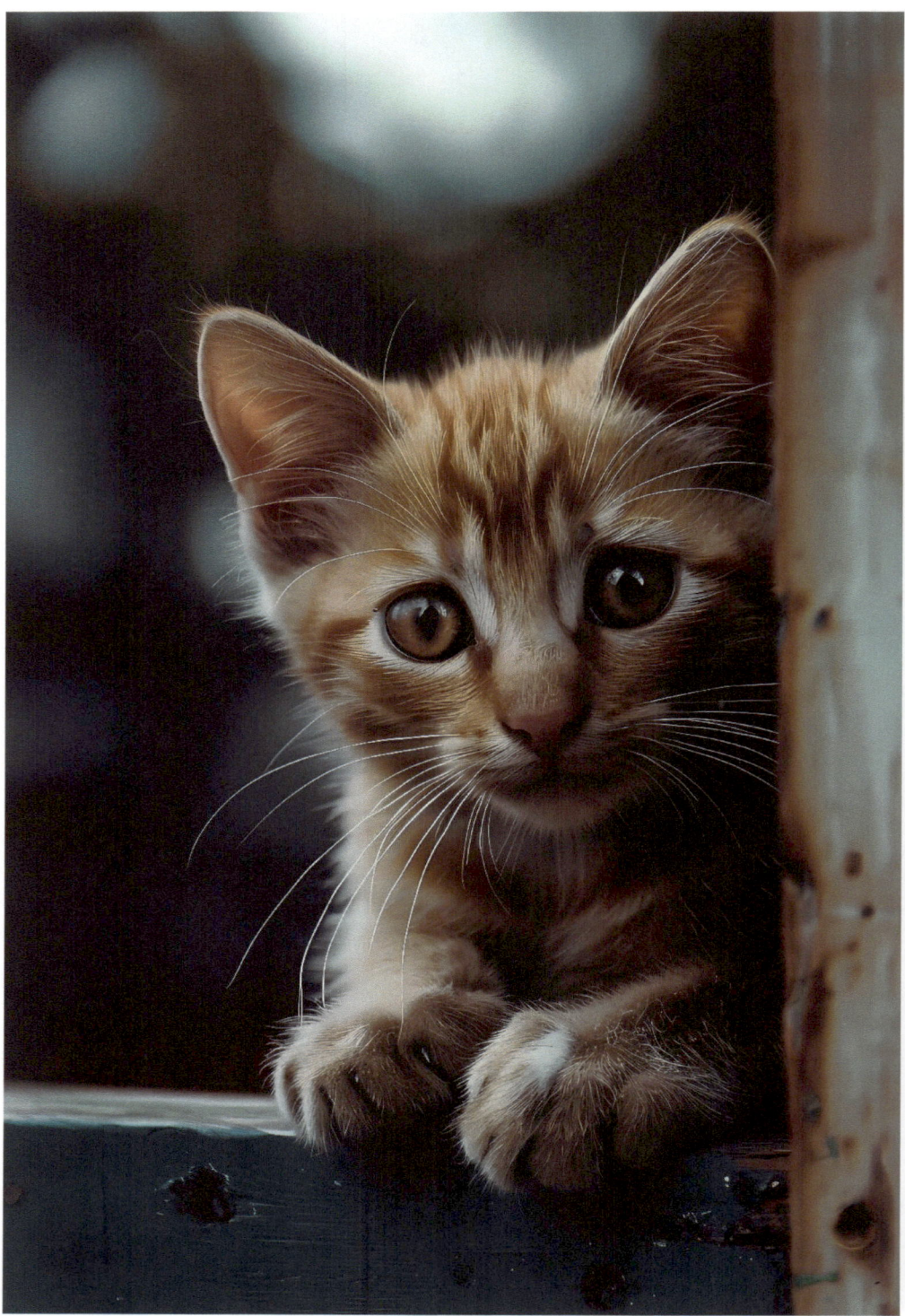

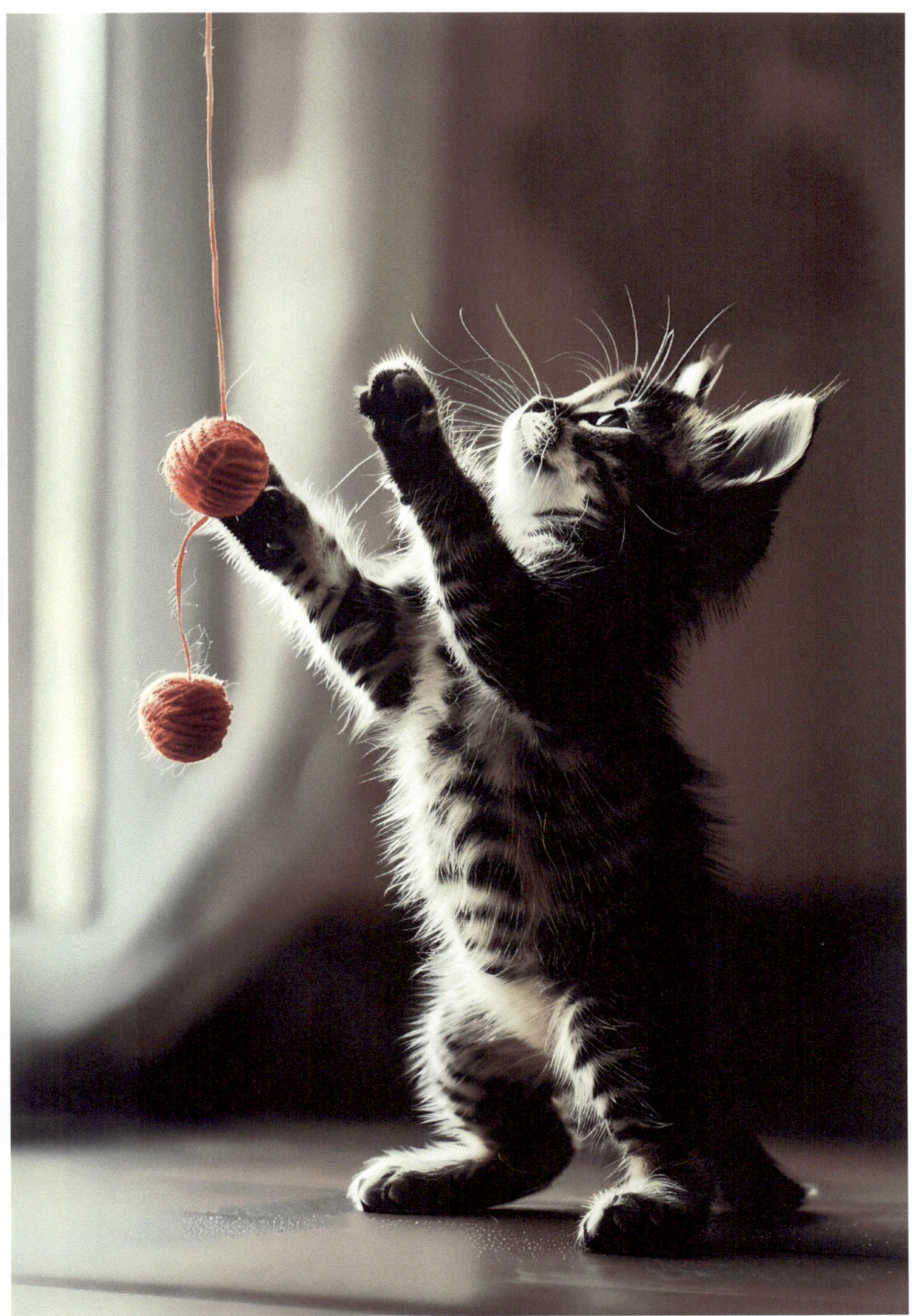

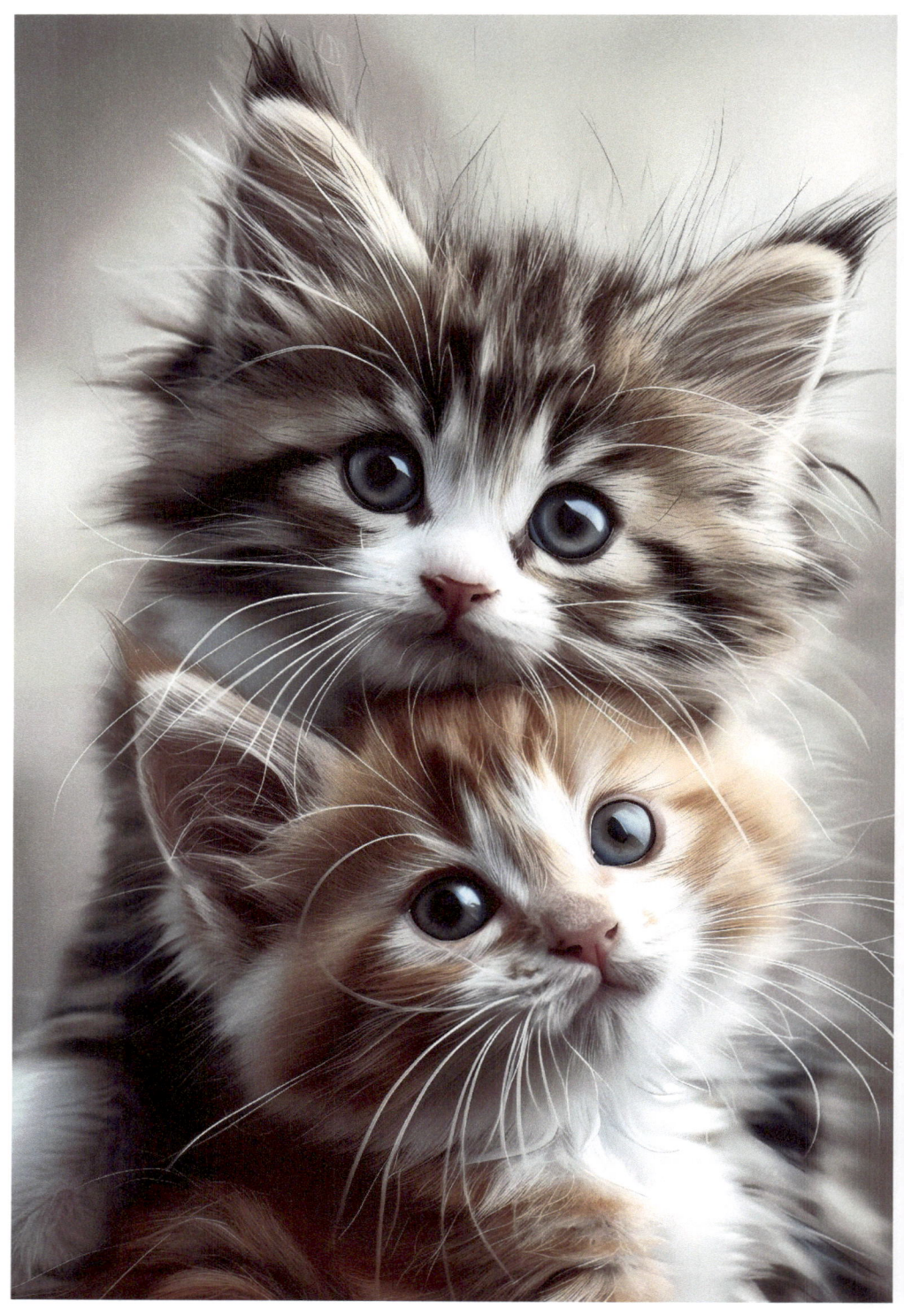

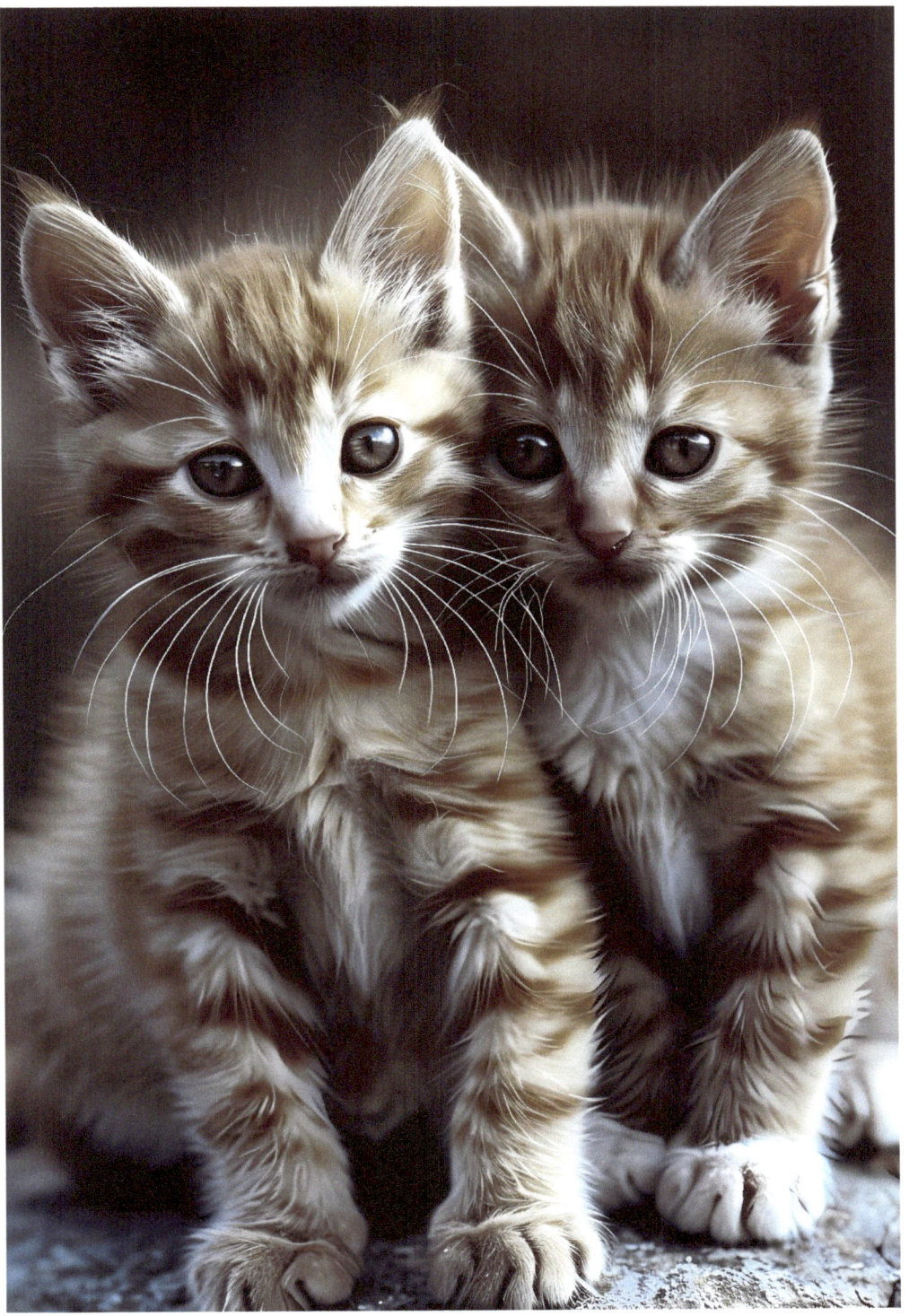

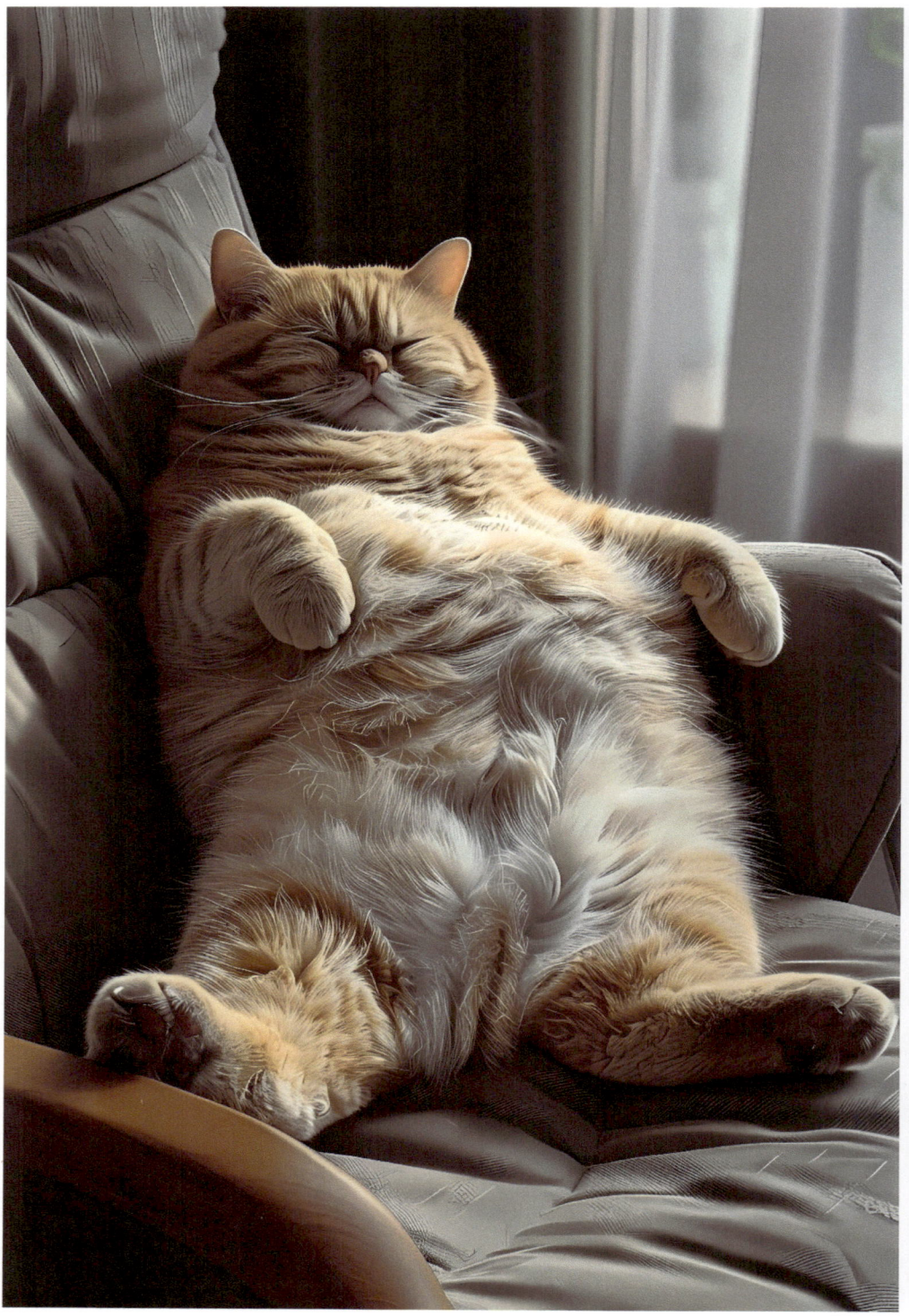

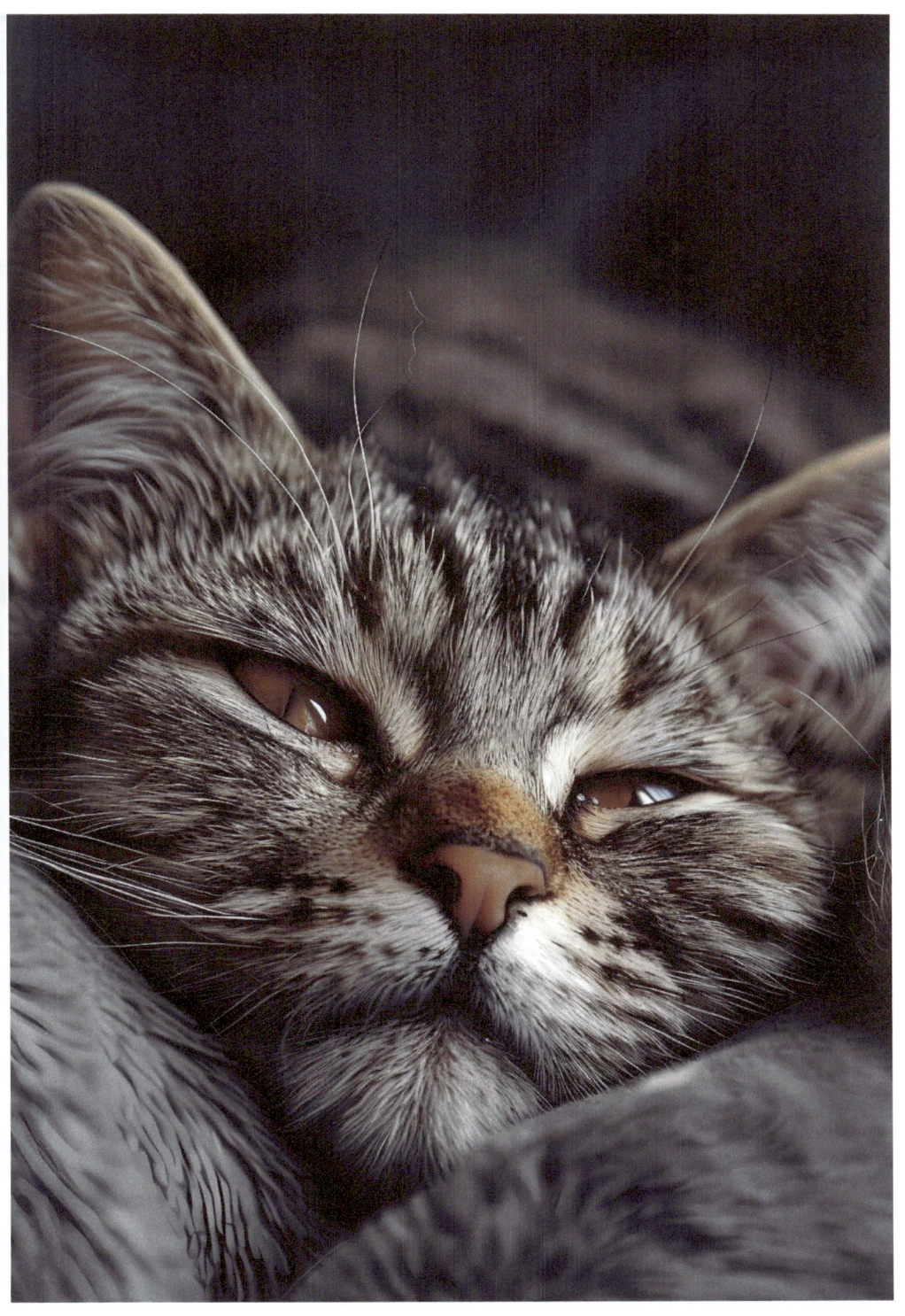

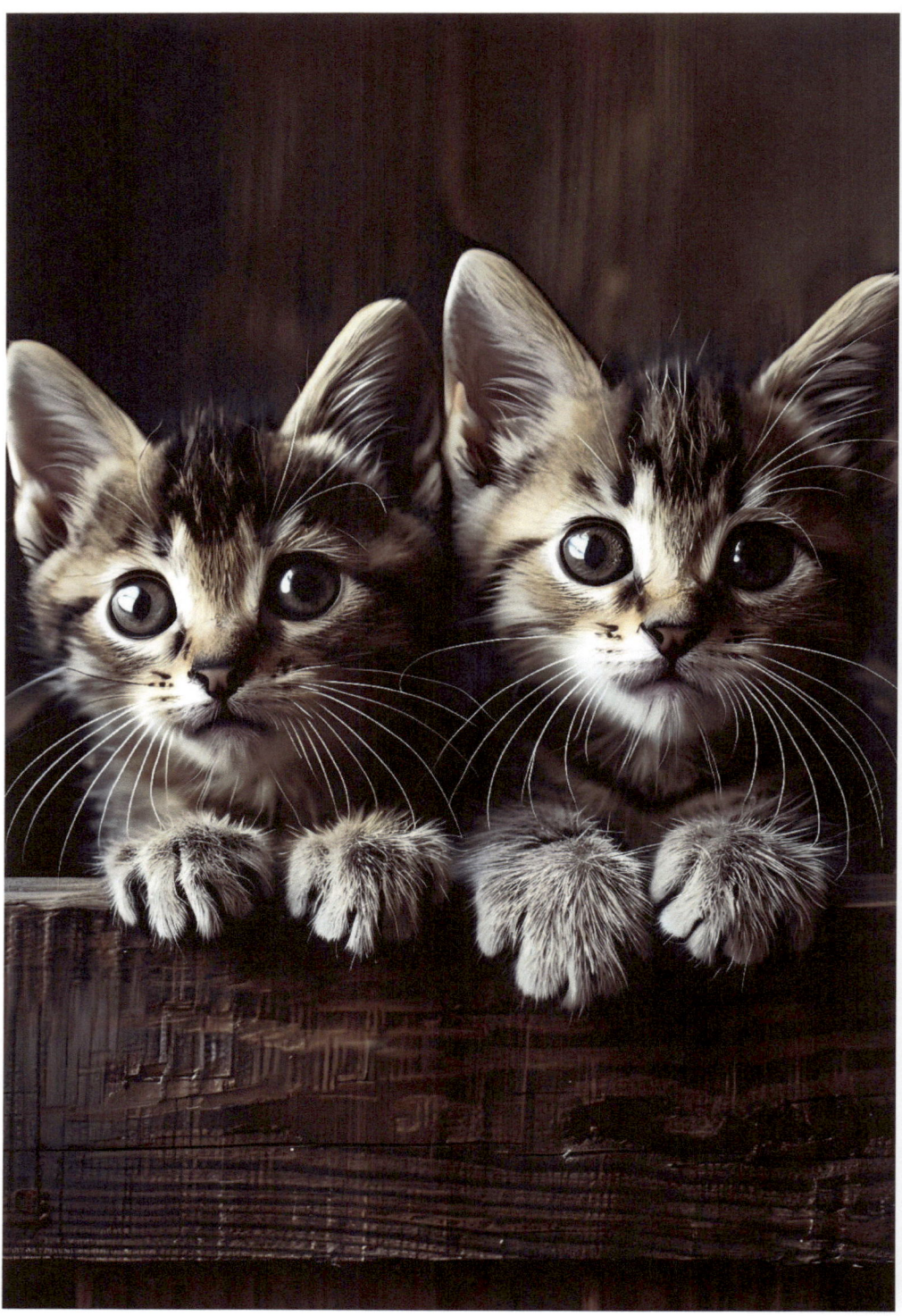

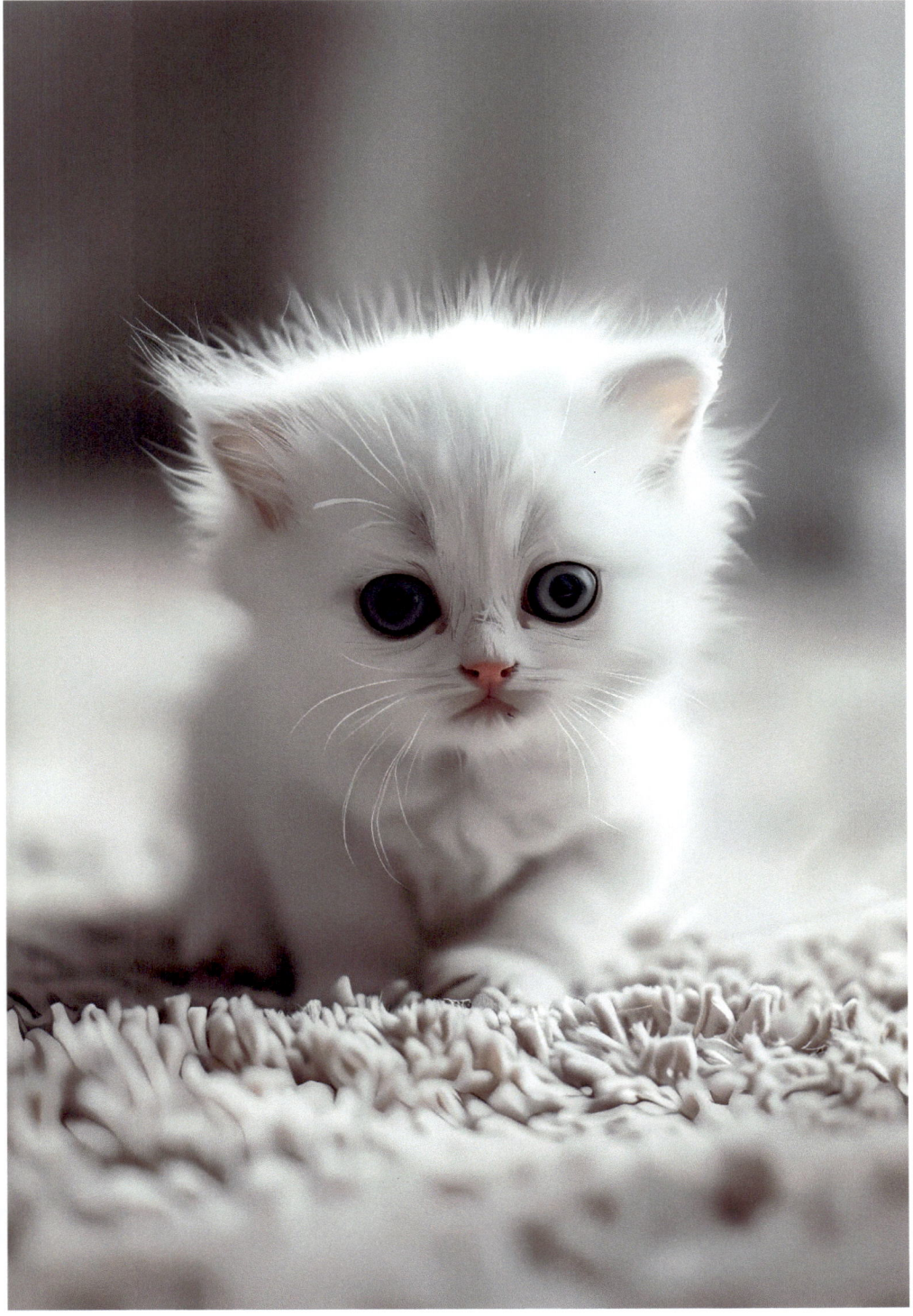

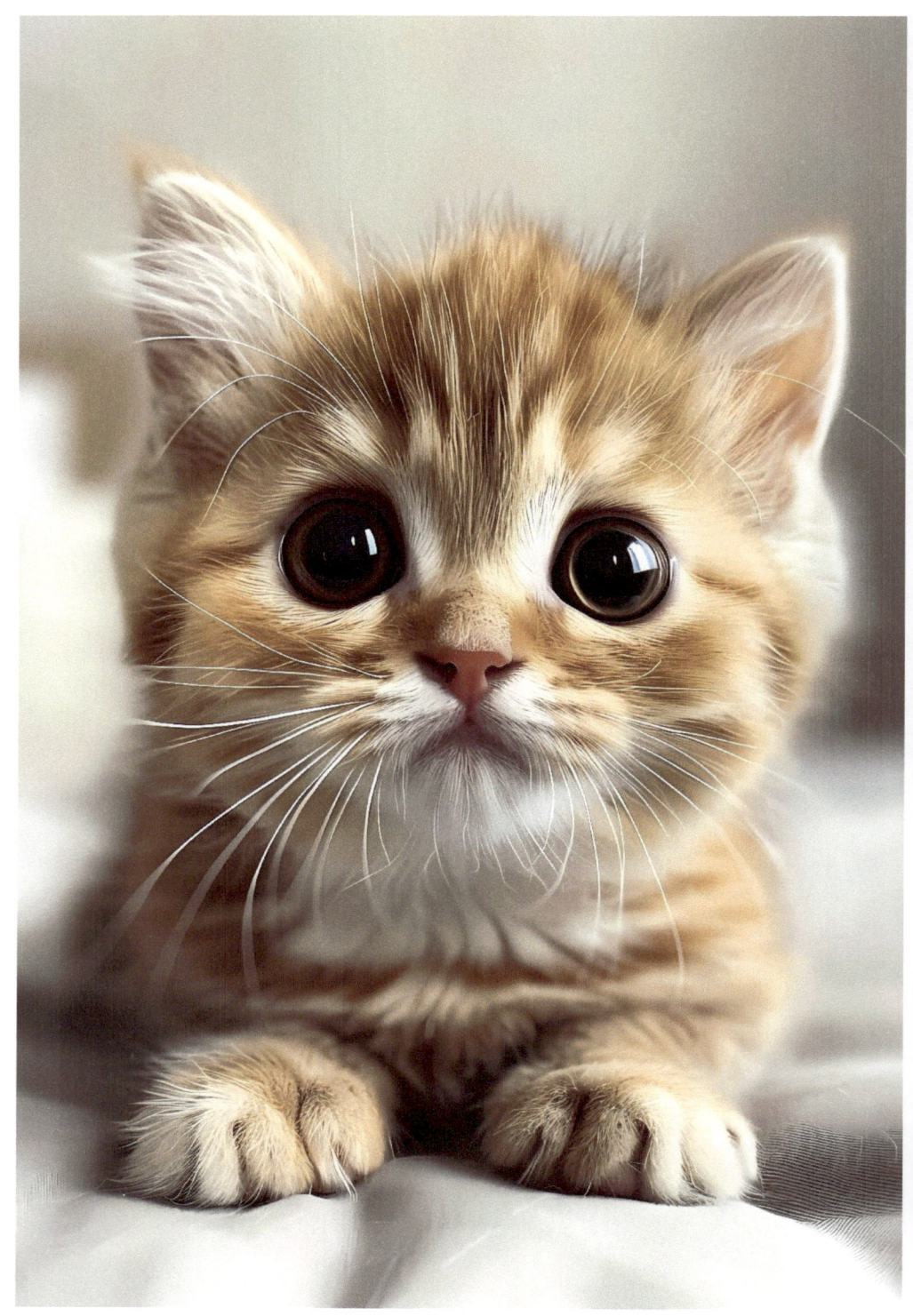

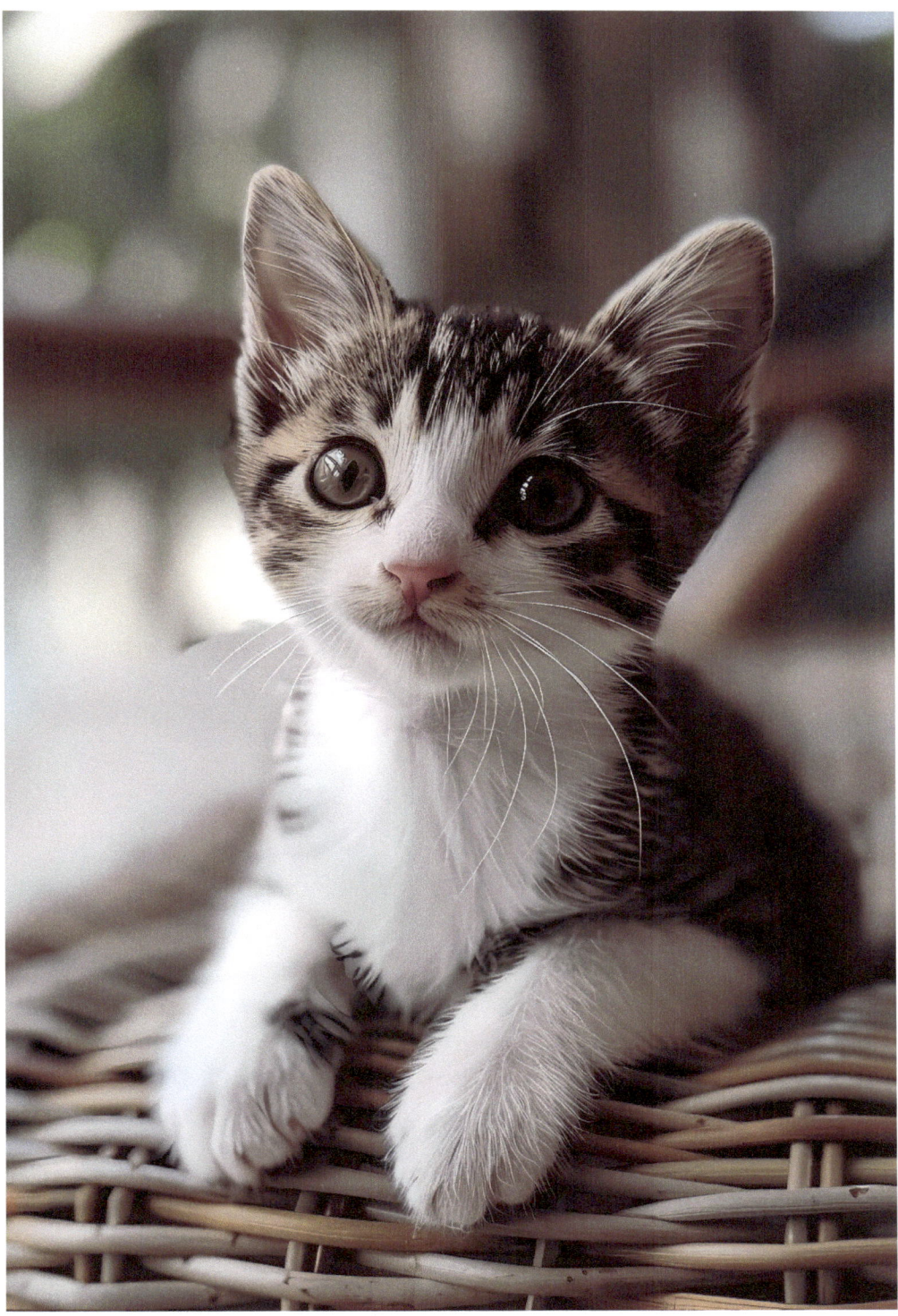

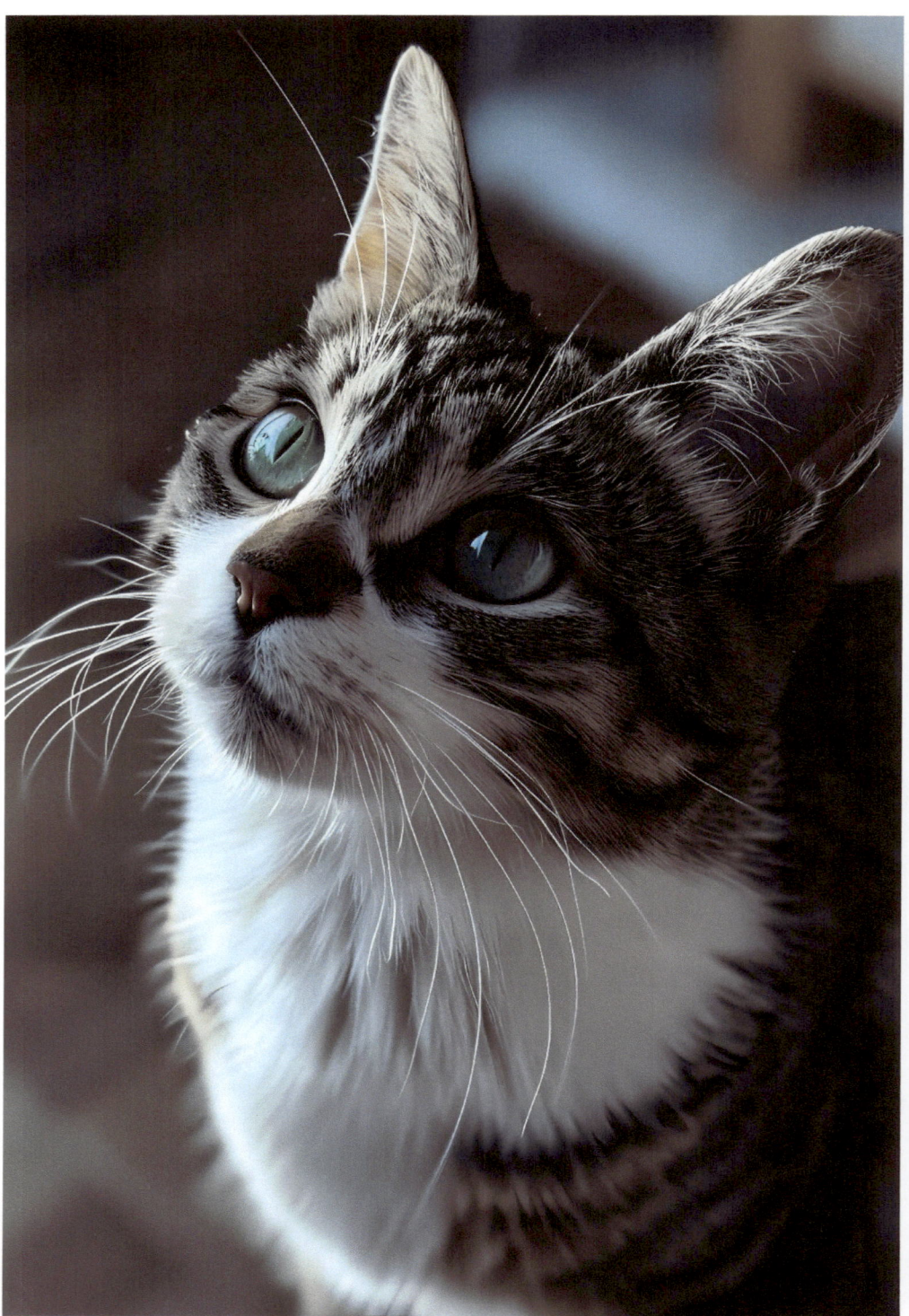

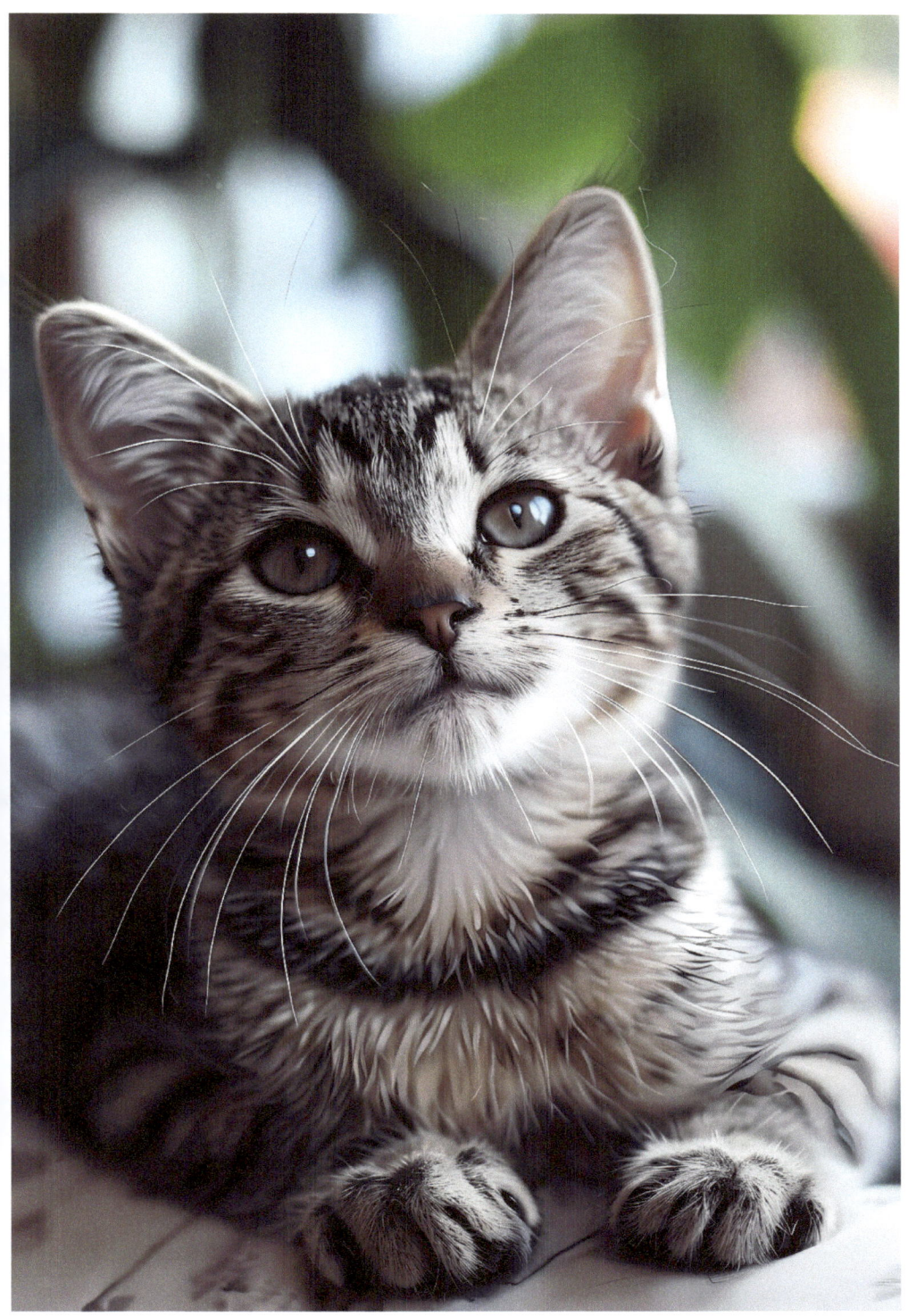

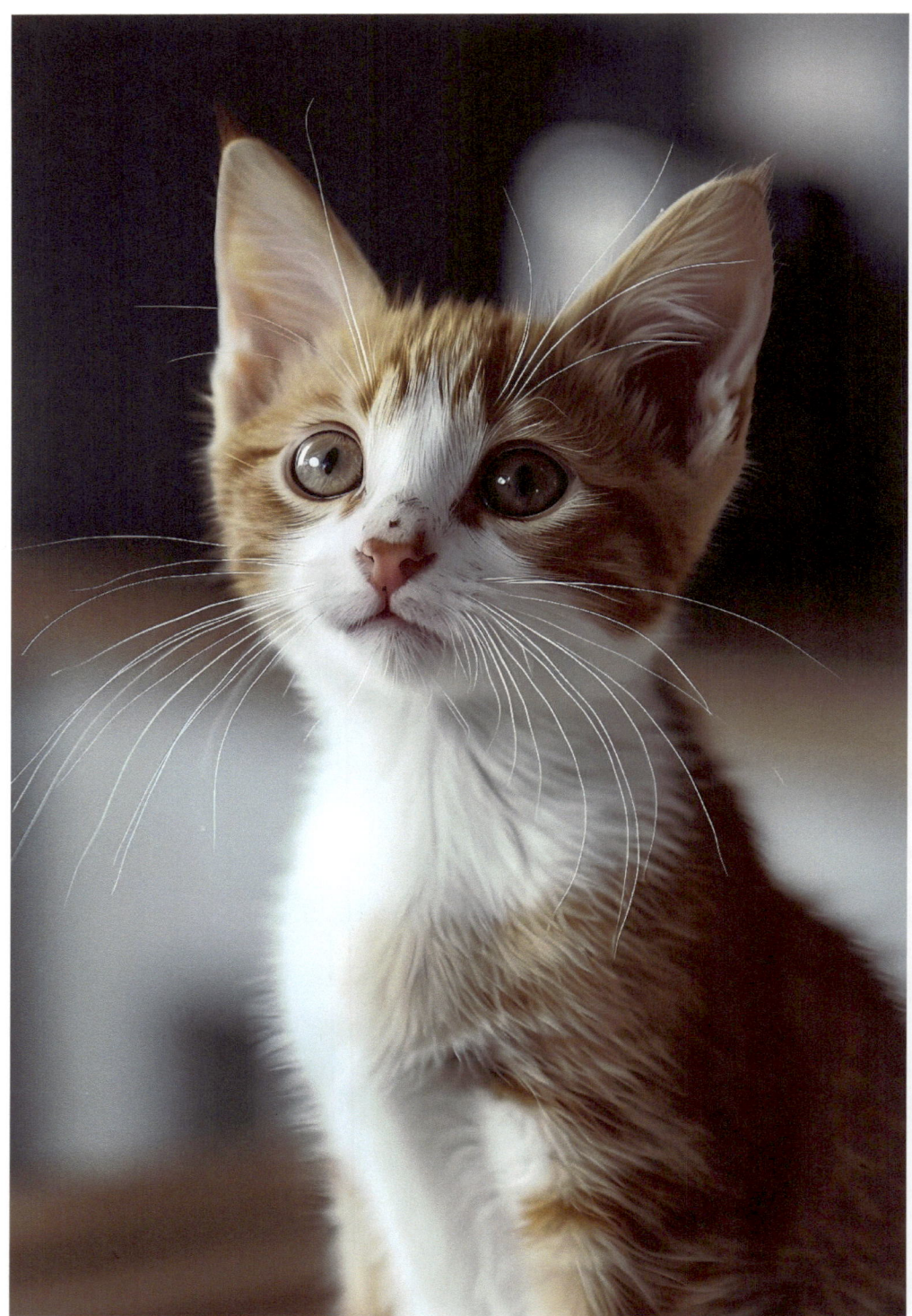

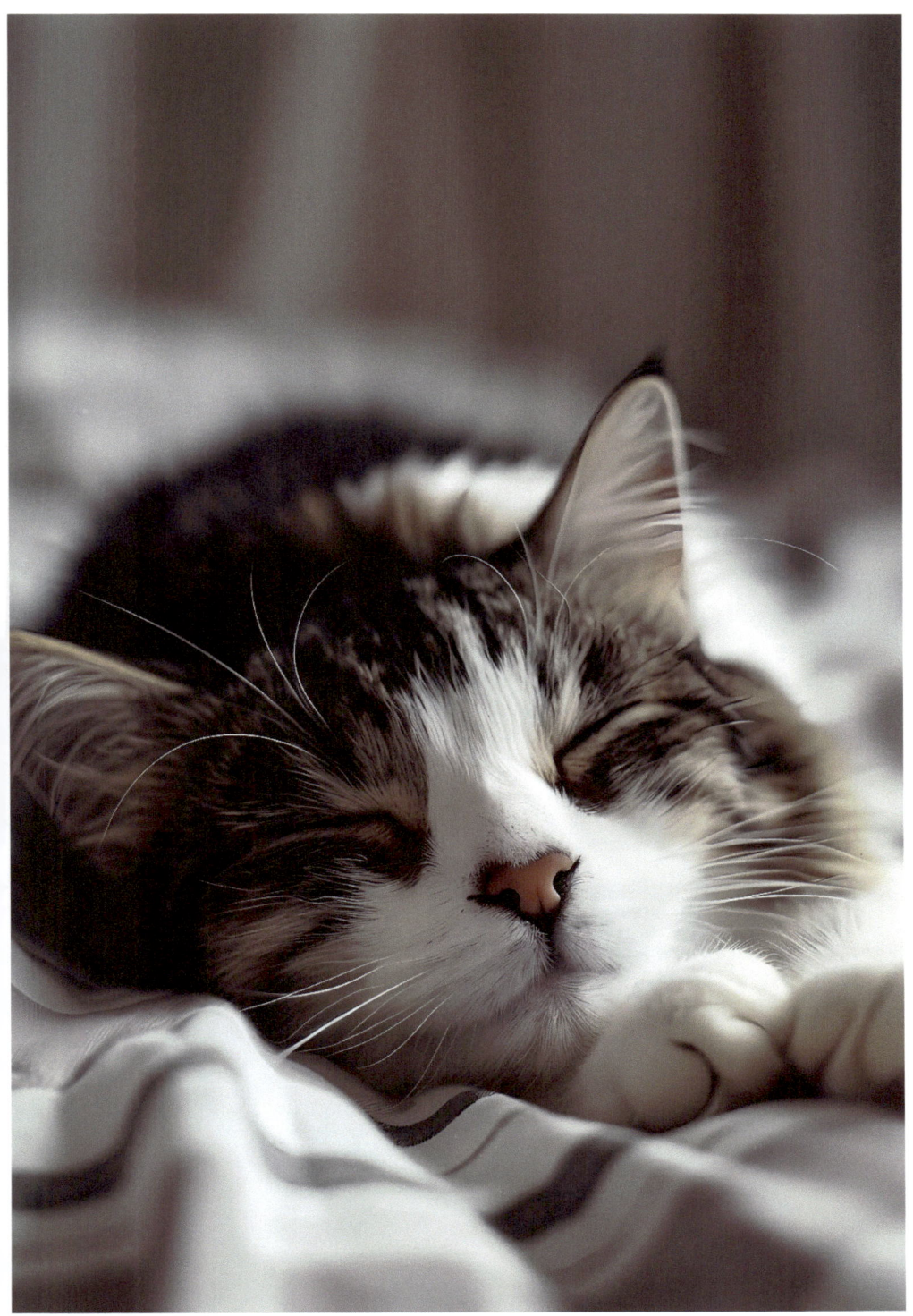

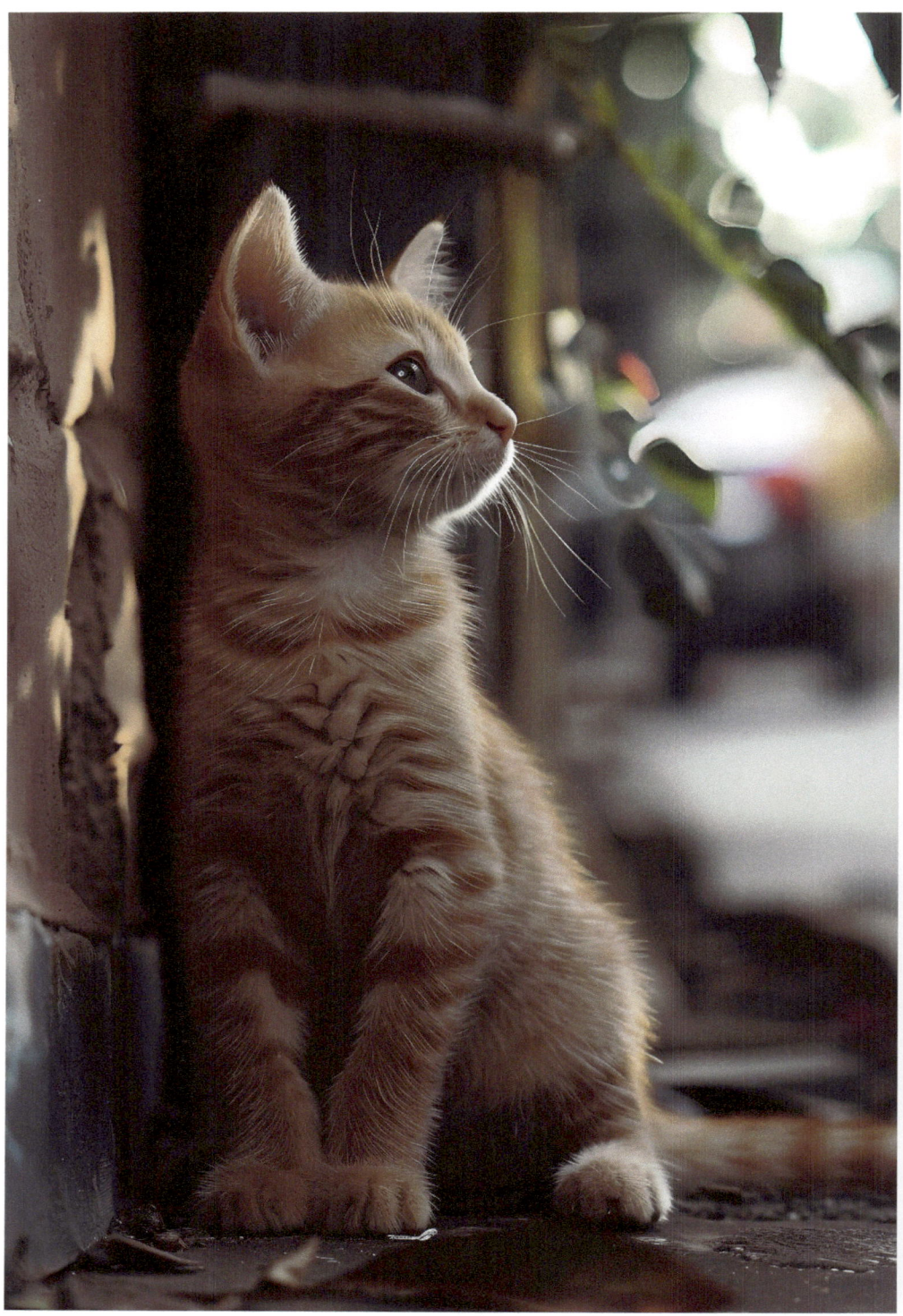

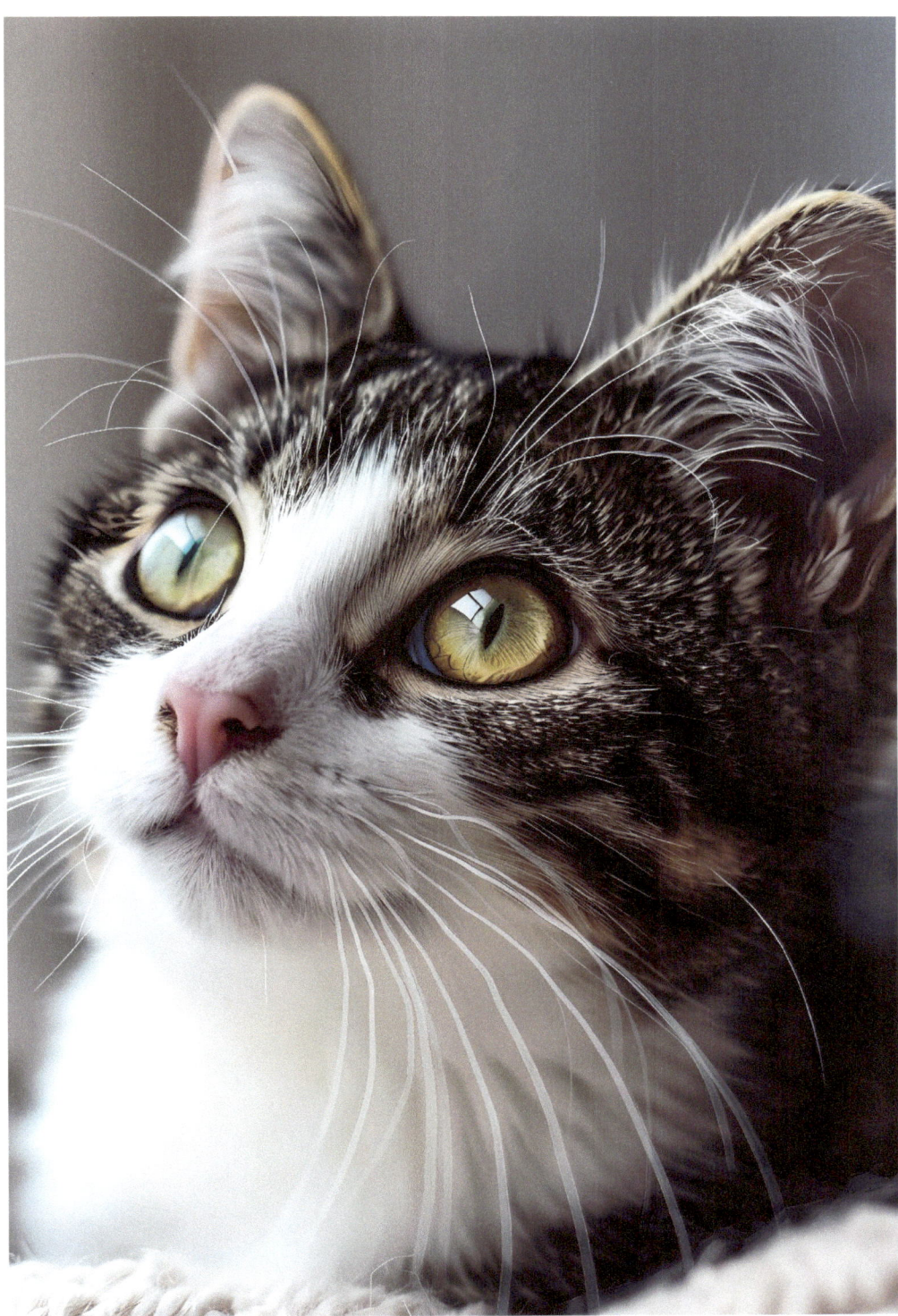

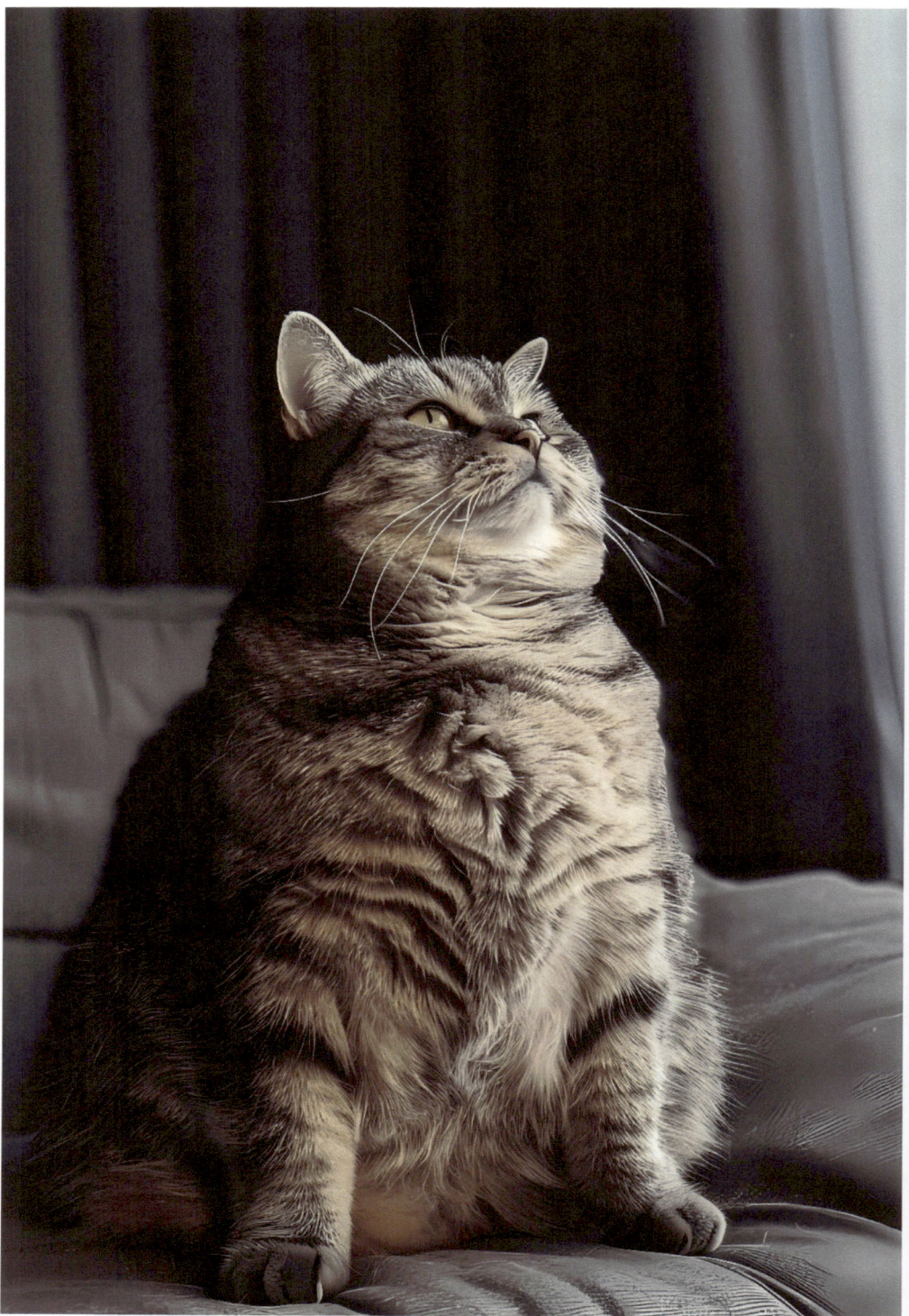

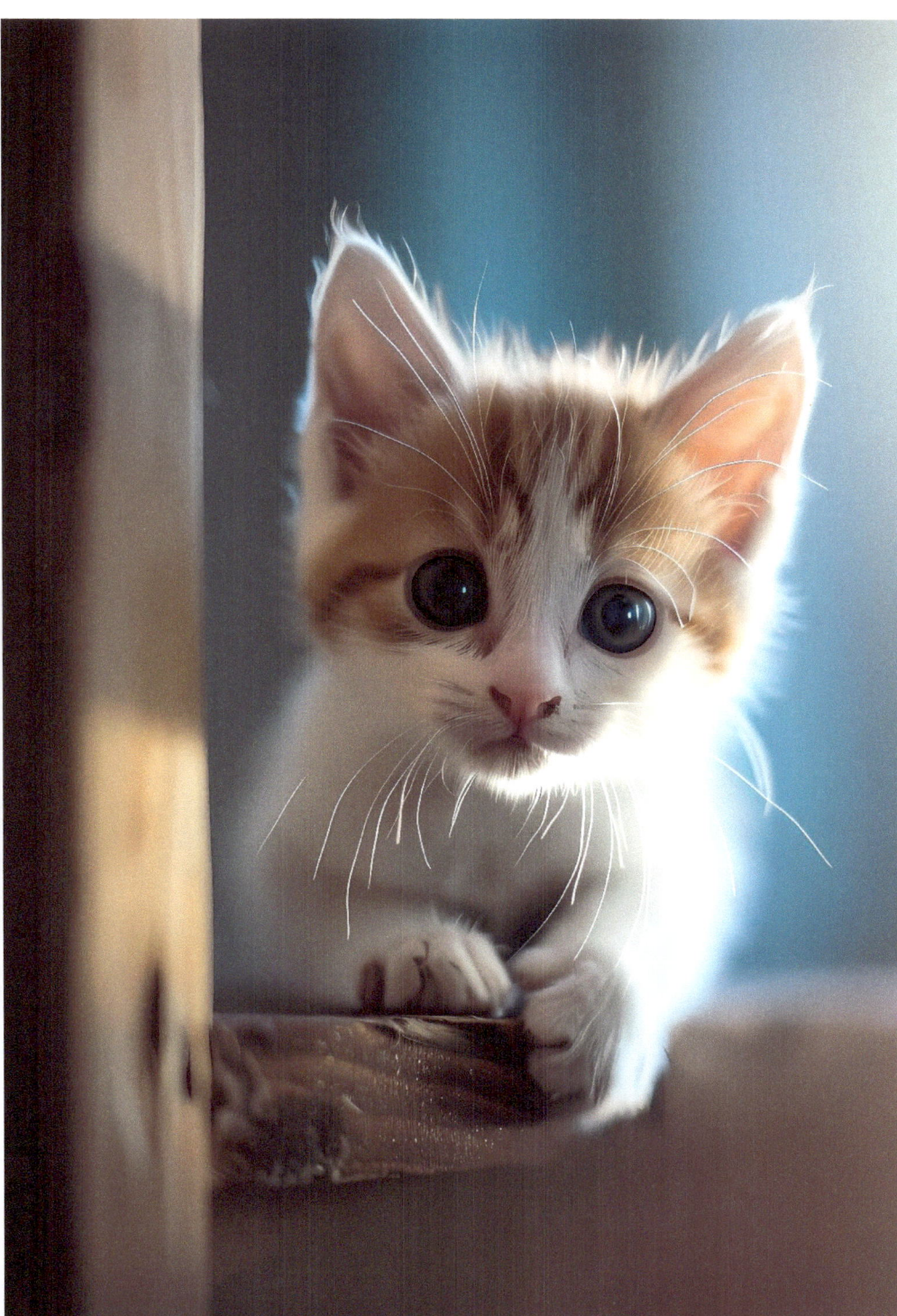

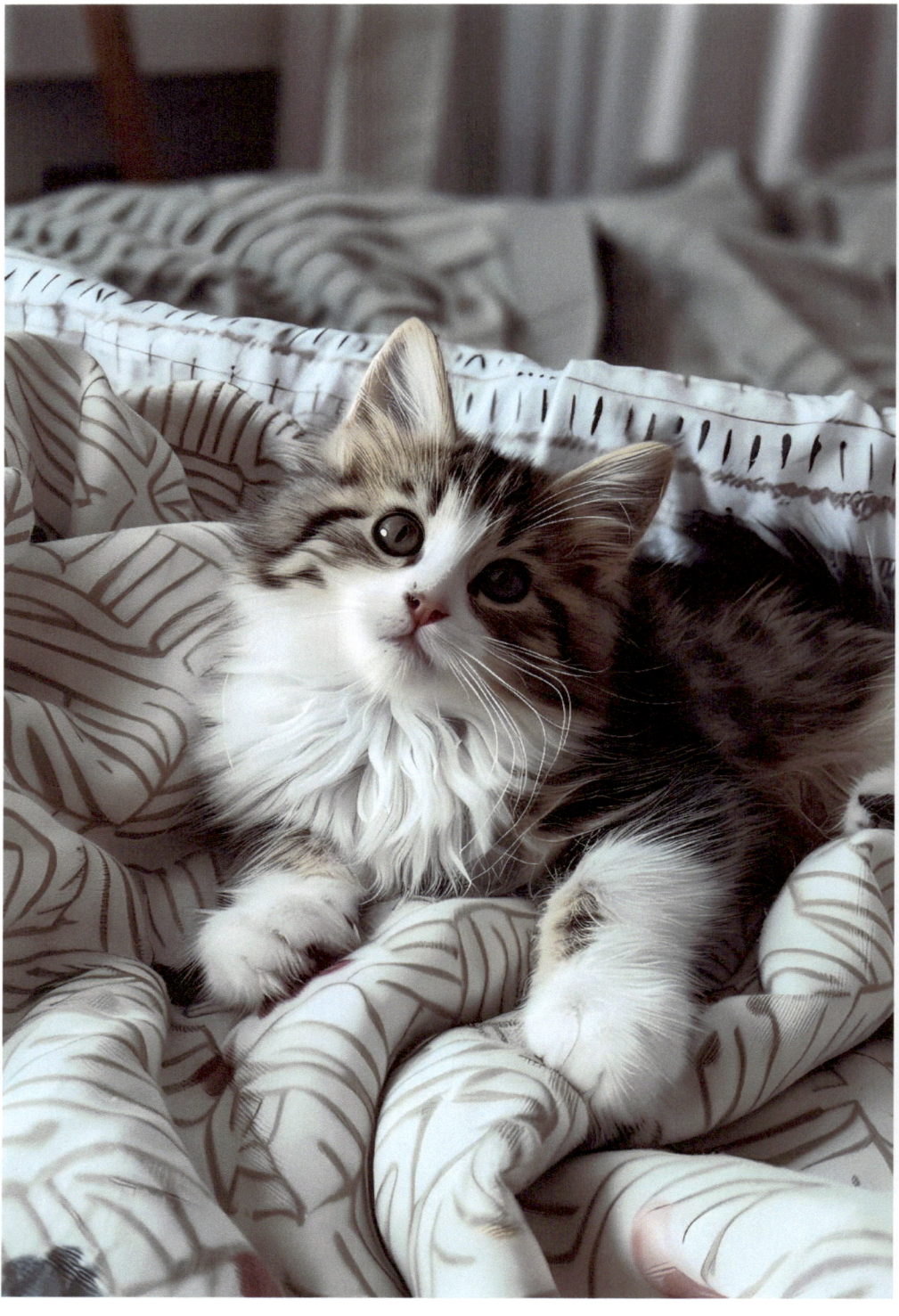

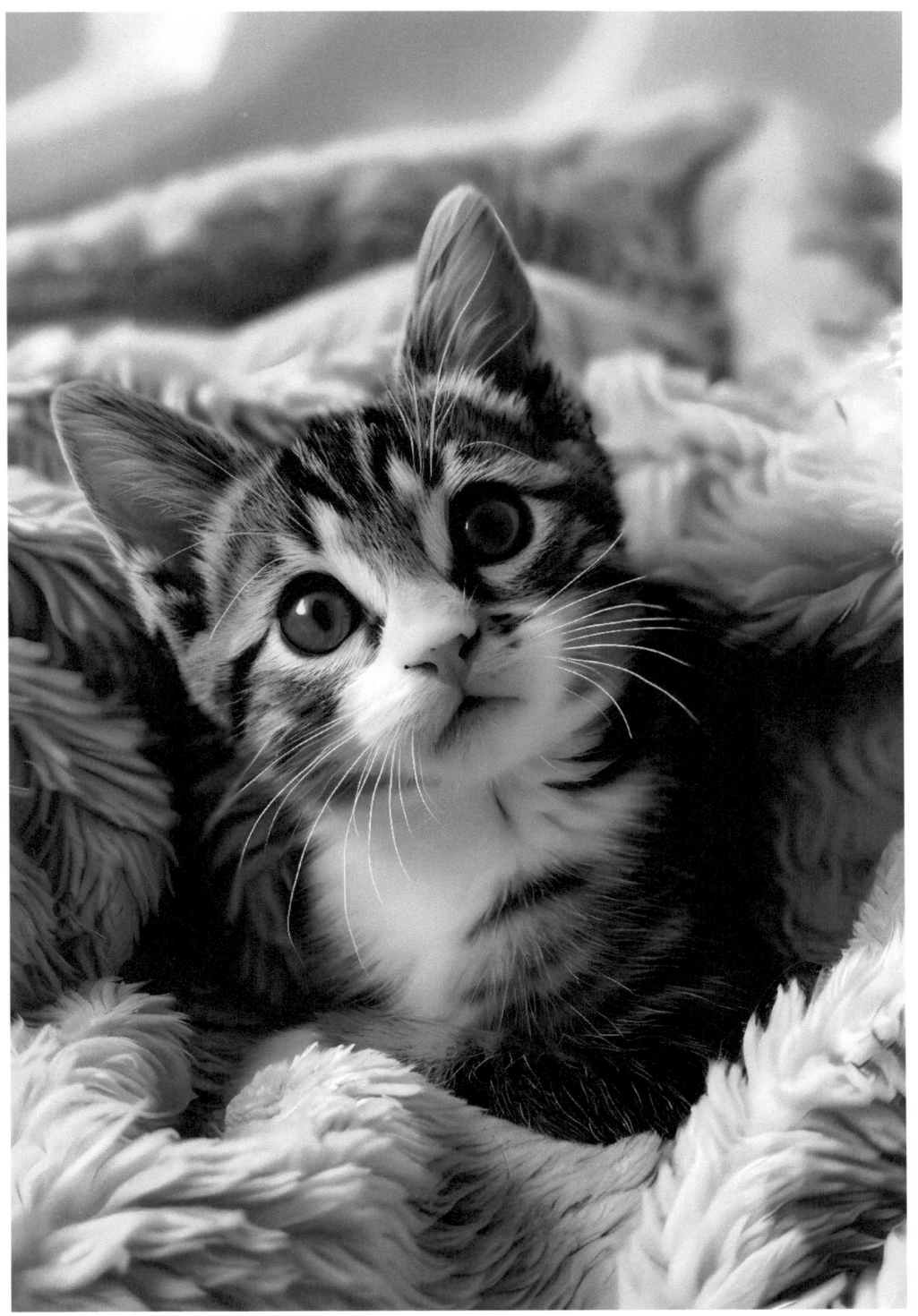

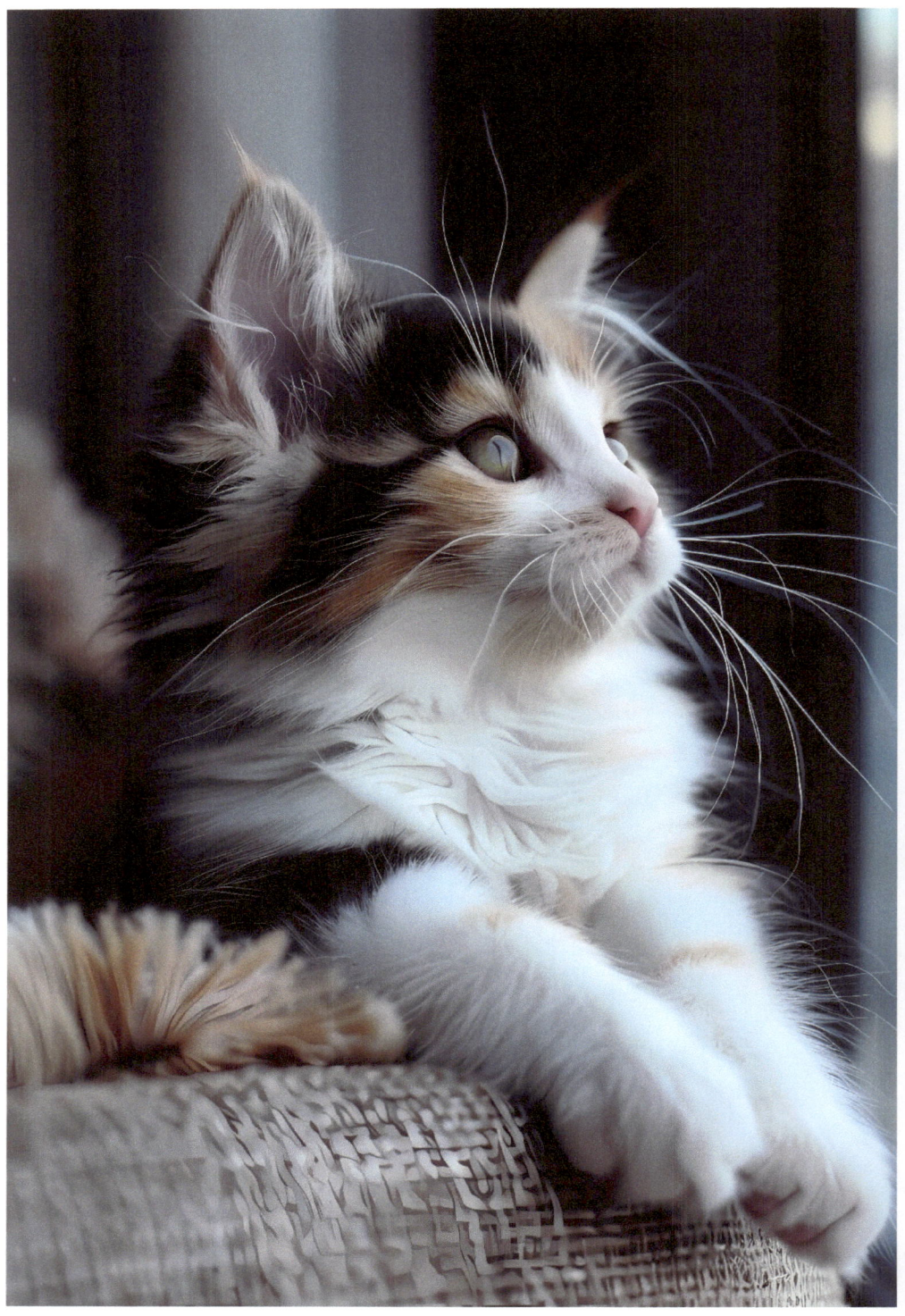

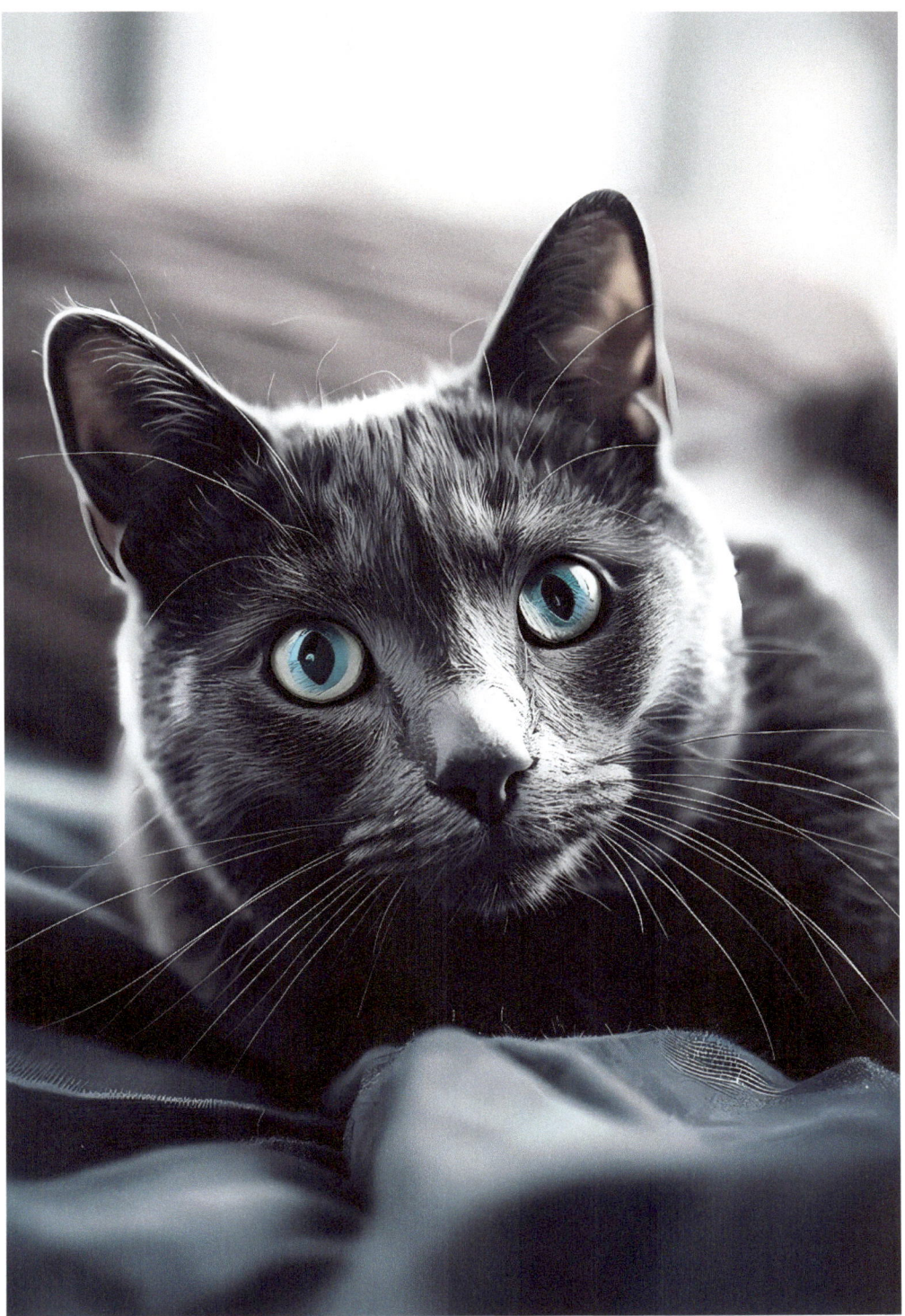

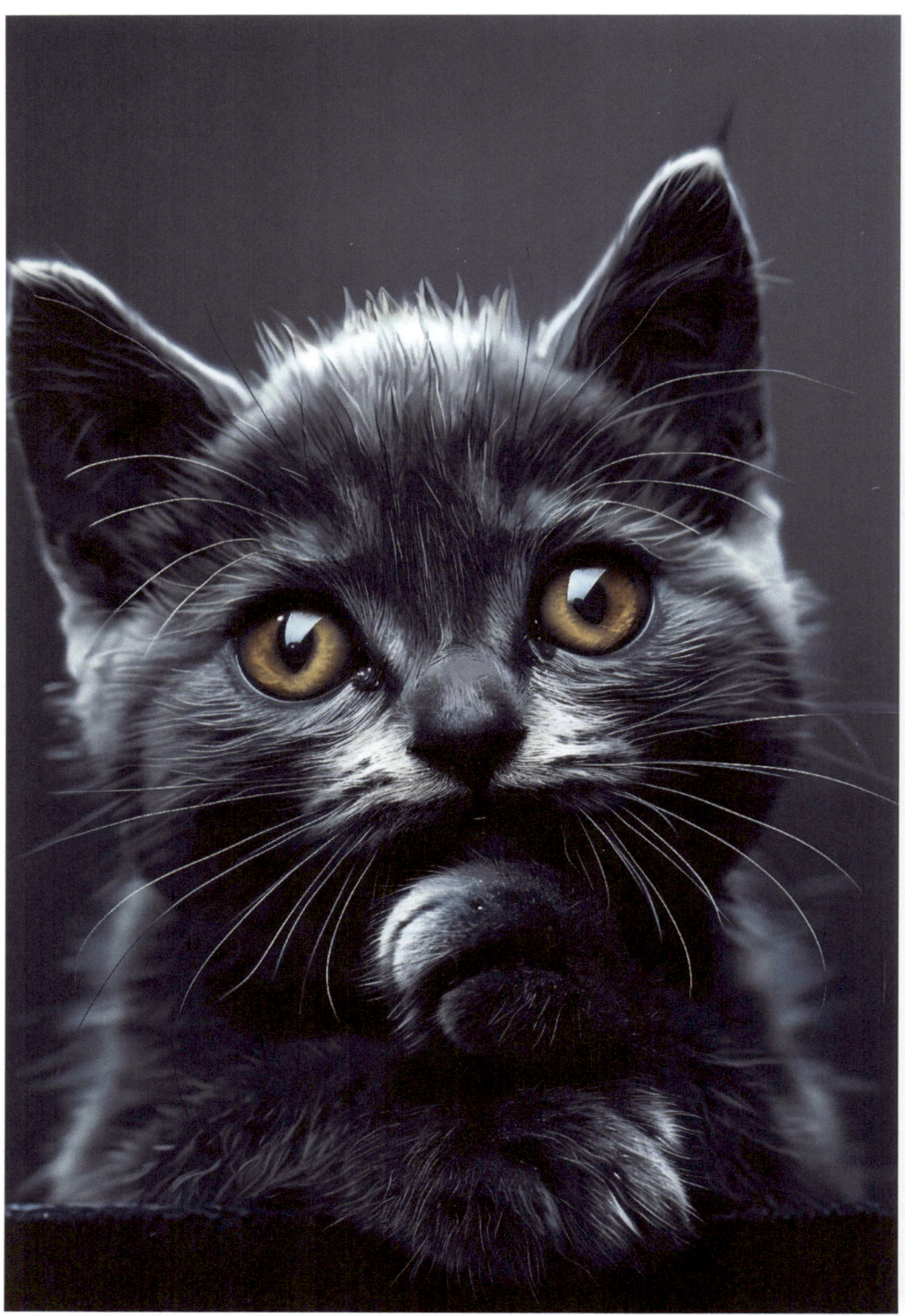

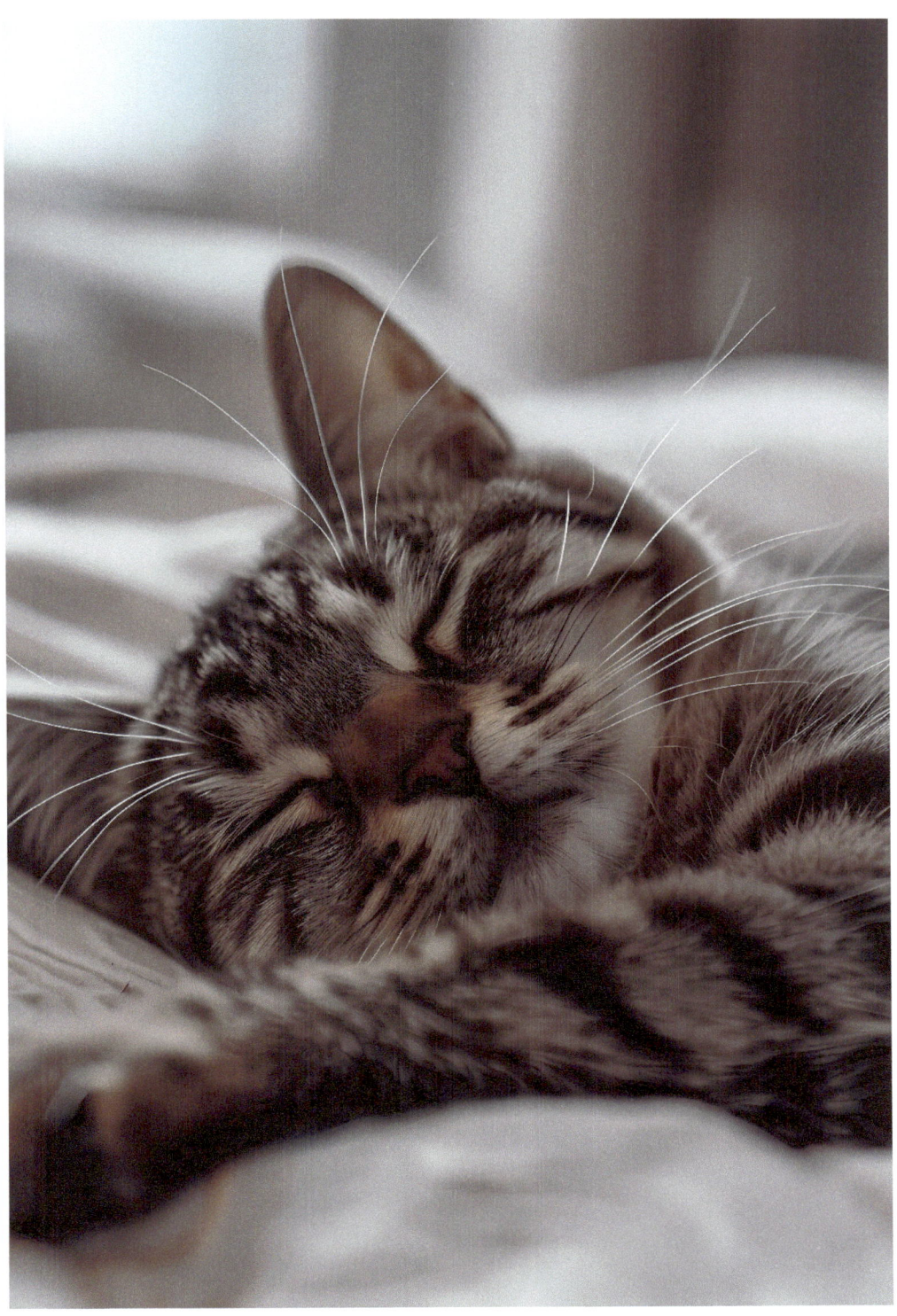

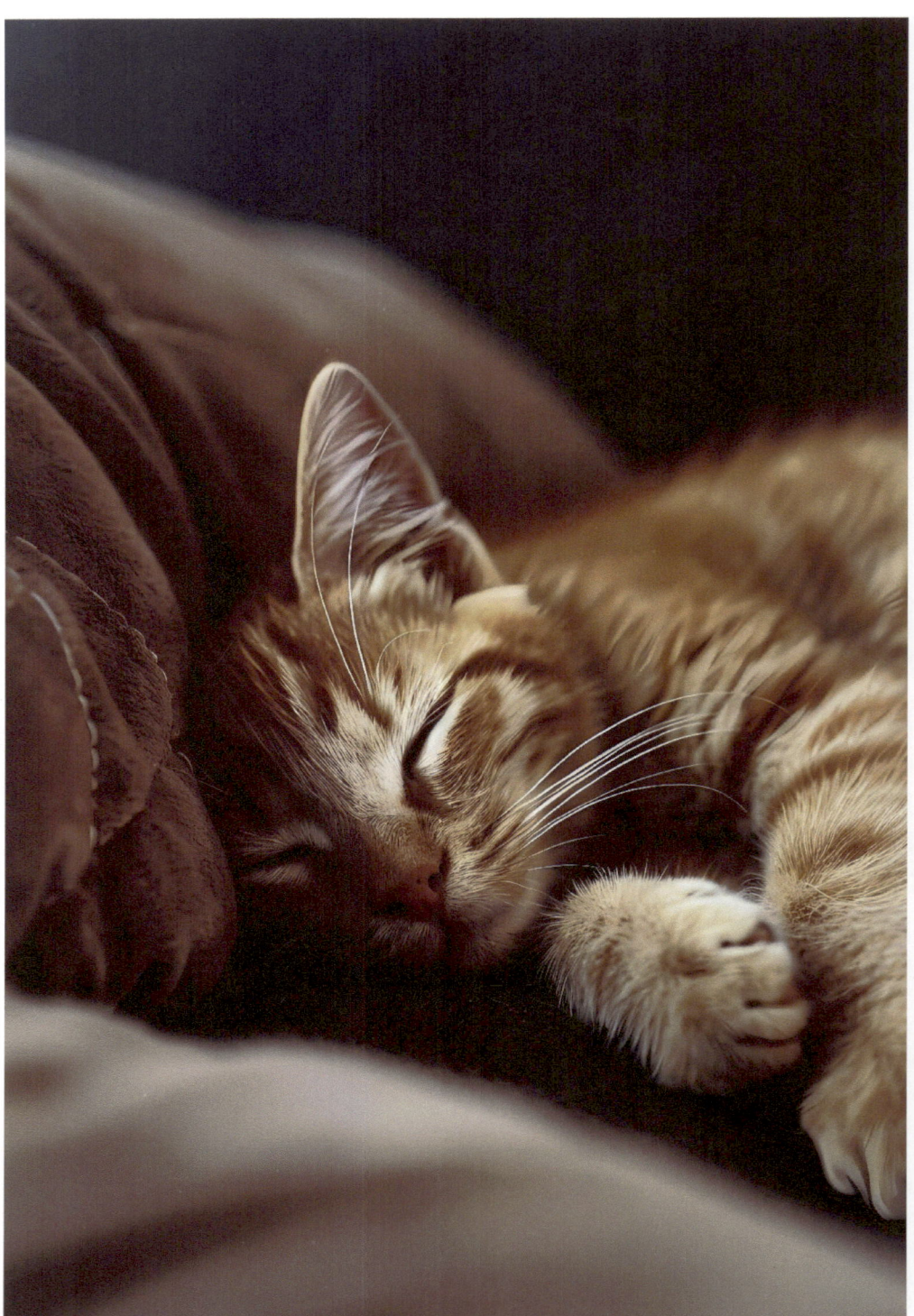

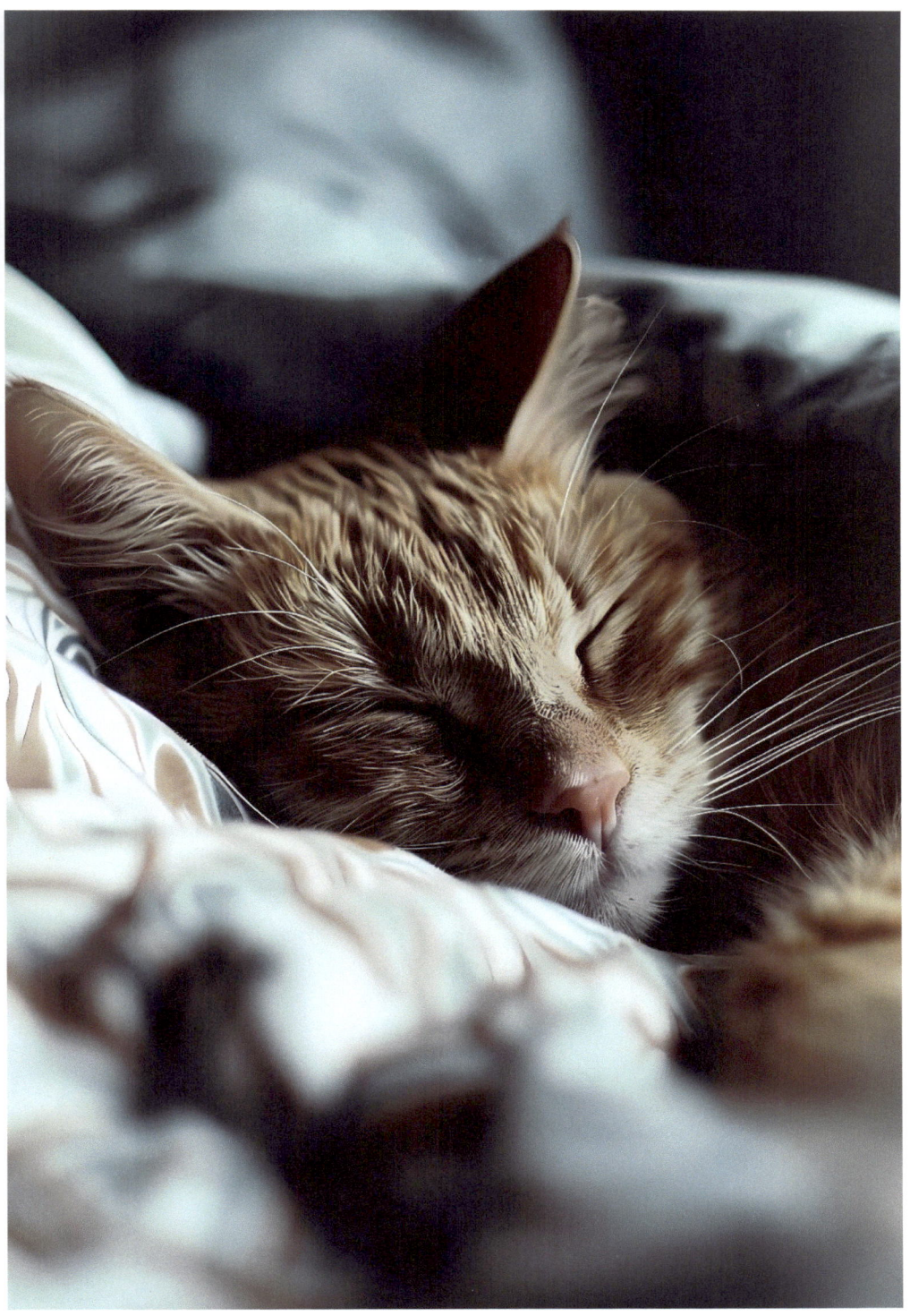

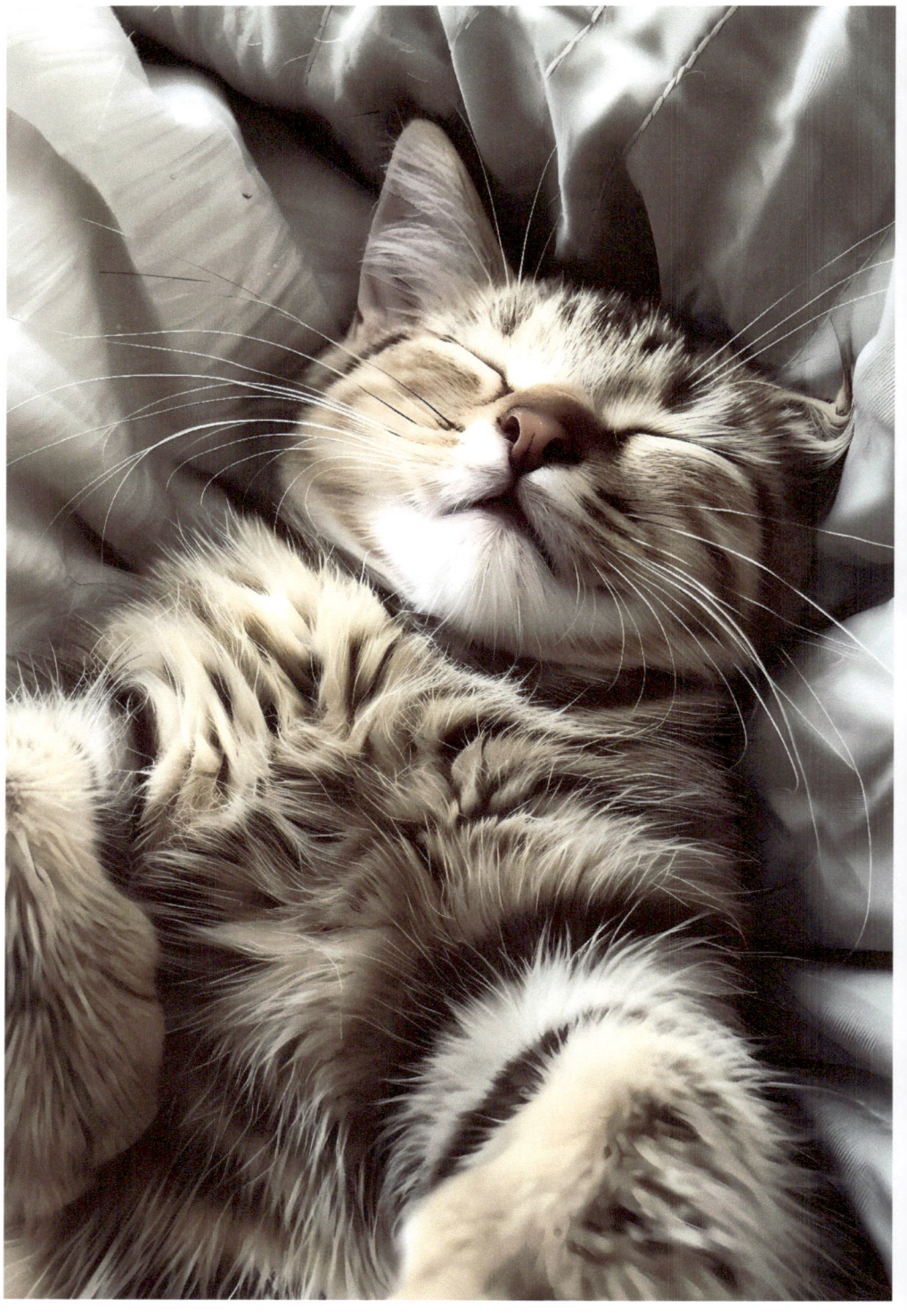

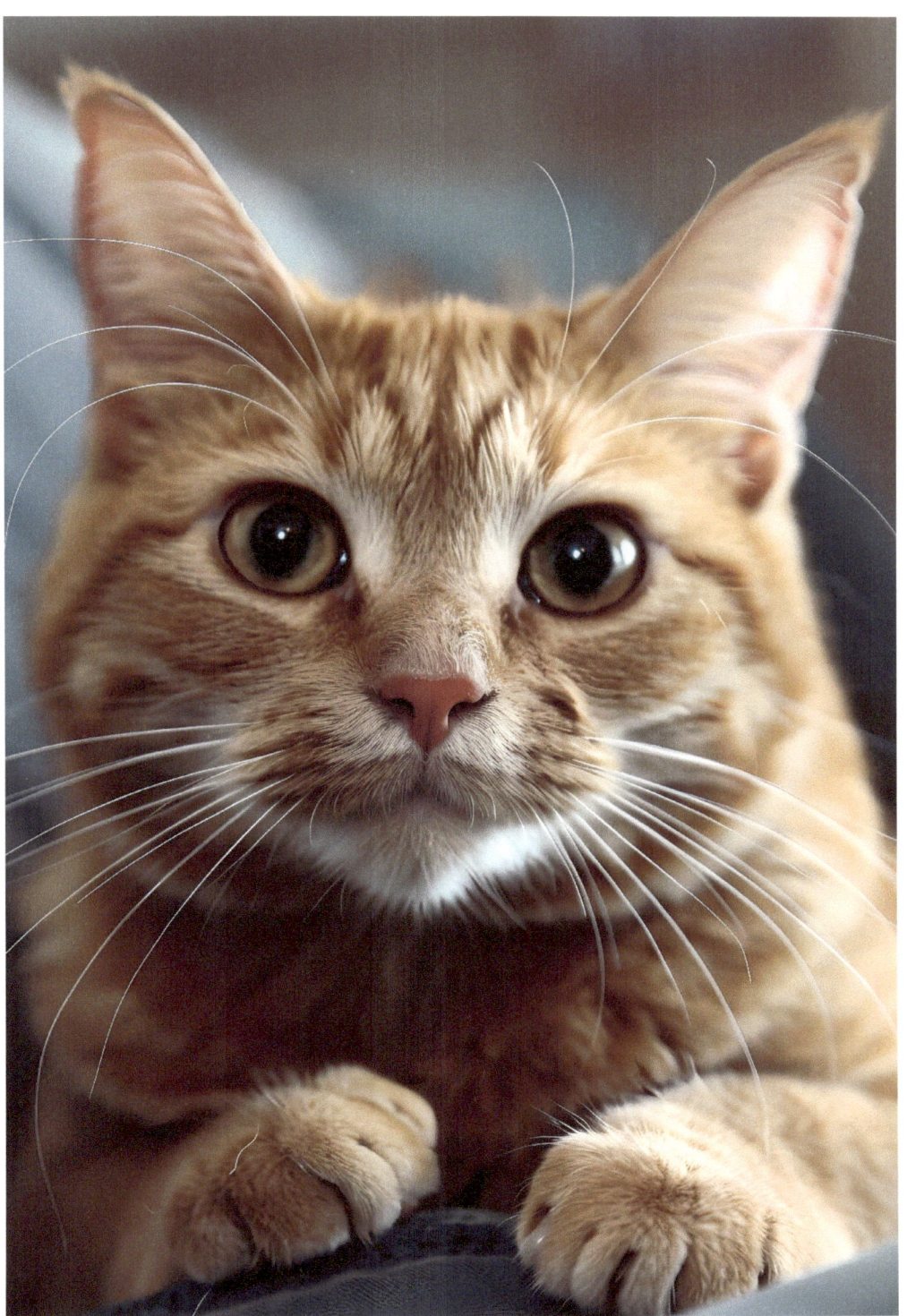

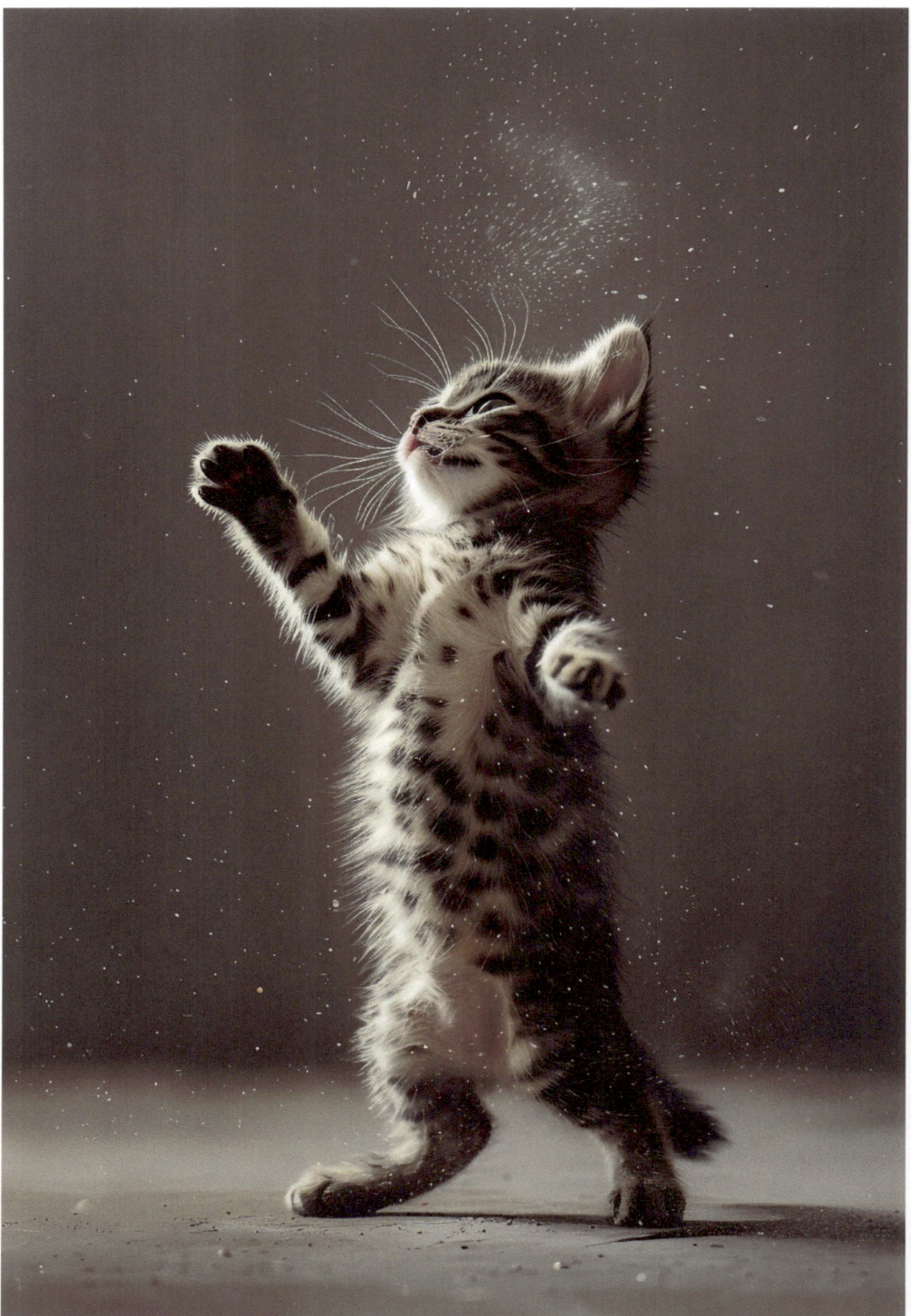

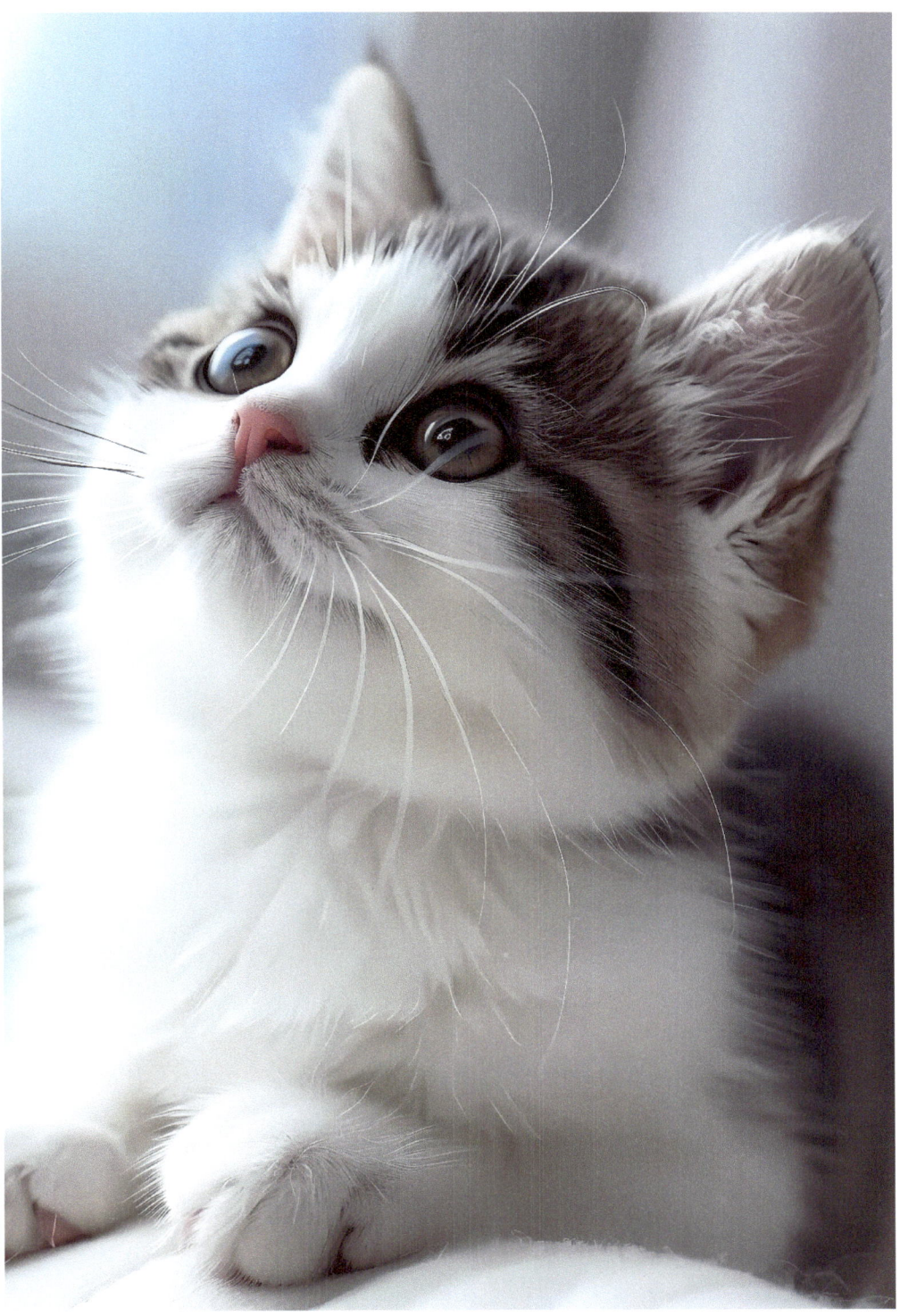

www.ingramcontent.com/pod-product-compliance
Lightning Source LLC
Chambersburg PA
CBHW040335220526
45473CB00009B/2691